SPORTS in AMERICA
1980–1989

MICHAEL TEITELBAUM

SERIES FOREWORD BY LARRY KEITH

Facts On File, Inc.

1980–1989
Sports in America

Copyright © 2004 Michael Teitelbaum
Foreword copyright © 2004 Larry Keith

Facts On File, Inc.
132 West 31st Street
New York NY 10001

Library of Congress Cataloging-in-Publication Data

Sports in America / produced by the Shoreline Publishing Group.
    v. cm.
Includes bibliographical references and indexes.
Contents: [1] 1910-1919 / by James Buckley, Jr. and John Walters — [2] 1920-1939 / by John Walters — [3] 1940-1949 / by Phil Barber — [4] 1950-1959 / by Jim Gigliotti — [5] 1960-1969 / by David Fischer — [6] 1970-1979 / by Timothy J. Seeberg and Jim Gigliotti — [7] 1980-1989 / by Michael Teitelbaum — [8] 1990-2003 / by Bob Woods.

ISBN 0-8160-5233-6 (hc : set : alk. paper) — ISBN 0-8160-5234-4 (hc : v. 1 : alk. paper) — ISBN 0-8160-5235-2 (hc : v. 2 : alk. paper) — ISBN 0-8160-5236-0 (hc : v. 3 : alk. paper) — ISBN 0-8160-5237-9 (hc : v. 4 : alk. paper) — ISBN 0-8160-5238-7 (hc : v. 5 : alk. paper) — ISBN 0-8160-5239-5 (hc : v. 6 : alk. paper) — ISBN 0-8160-5240-9 (hc : v. 7 :alk. paper) — ISBN 0-8160-5241-7 (hc : v. 8 : alk. paper)

1. Sports—United States—History.   I. Buckley, James, 1963-   . II. Shoreline Publishing Group. III. Facts on File, Inc.

GV583.S6826 2004
796'.0973'0904—dc22

2004004276

Facts On File books are available at special discounts when purchased in bulk quantities for businesses, associations, institutions, or sales promotions. Please call our Special Sales Department in New York at (212) 967-8800 or (800) 322-8755.

You can find Facts On File on the World Wide Web at http://www.factsonfile.com

Produced by the Shoreline Publishing Group LLC
President/Editorial Director: James Buckley Jr.
Contributing Editors: Jim Gigliotti, Beth Adelman
Text design by Thomas Carling, Carling Design, Inc.
Cover design by Pehrsson Design and Cathy Rincon
Index by Nanette Cardon, IRIS

Photo credits: Page 1: Courtesy Sports Immortals, Inc. Hockey star Wayne Gretzky, known to fans around the world simply as the "Great One," rewrote his sport's record book with the most prolific scoring season in history in 1981–82 (see page 27). Gretzky's famous number-99 jersey is autographed in this photo. All interior photos courtesy AP/Wide World except for Corbis, pages 9, 16, 41, 51, 59, 60, 75, 89. Sports icons by Bob Eckstein.

Printed in the United States of America.

VH PKG 10 9 8 7 6 5 4 3 2 1

This book is printed on acid-free paper.

CONTENTS

Olympic gymnast Mary Lou Retton (page 47)

FOREWORD

BY LARRY KEITH

IN THE FALL OF 1984, STUDENTS AT COLUMBIA University's prestigious Graduate School of Journalism requested that a new course be added to the curriculum—sports journalism.

Sports journalism? In the graduate program of an Ivy League institution? Get serious.

But the students were serious, and, as students will do, they persisted. Eventually, the school formed a committee to interview candidates for the position of "adjunct professor." As it happened, though, the committee wasn't just looking for a professional sports journalist to teach the course part time. That august body wanted to hear clear and convincing arguments that the course should be offered at all.

In other words, did sports matter? And, more to the point, should an institution that administered the Pulitzer Prize, the highest award in journalism, associate itself with the coverage of "fun and games?"

Two decades later, I am pleased to say that Columbia did decide to offer the course and that it remains in the curriculum. With modest pride, I confess that I helped make the arguments that swayed the committee and became the new adjunct professor.

I reflected on that experience when the *Sports in America* editors invited me to write the Foreword to this important series. I said then, and I say now, "Sport is an integral part of American society and requires the attention of a competent and vigilant press." For our purposes here, I might also add, "because it offers insights to our history and culture."

Sports in America is much more than a compilation of names, dates, and facts. Each volume chronicles accomplishments, advances, and expansions of the possible. Not just in the physical ability to run faster, jump higher, or hit a ball farther, but in the cognitive ability to create goals and analyze how to achieve them. In this way, sports, the sweaty offspring of recreation and competition, resemble any other field of endeavor. I certainly wouldn't equate the race for a gold medal with the race to the moon, but the essentials are the same: the application of talent, determination, research, practice, and hard work to a meaningful objective.

Sports matter because they represent the best and worst of us. They give us flesh-and-blood examples of courage and skill. They often embody a heroic human interest story, about overcoming poverty, injustice, injury, or disease. The phrase, "Sports is a microcosm of life," could also be, "Life is a microcosm of sports." Consider racial issues, for example. When Jackie Robinson of the Brooklyn Dodgers broke through Major League Baseball's color barrier in 1947, the significance extended beyond the national pastime. Precisely because baseball *was* the national pastime, this important event reverberated throughout American society.

To be sure, black stars from individual sports had preceded him (notably Joe Louis in boxing and Jesse Owens in track and field), and others would follow (Arthur Ashe in tennis and Tiger Woods in golf), but Robinson stood out as an important member of a *team*. He wasn't just playing with the Dodgers, he was traveling with them, dressing with them, eating with them, living with them. The benefits of integration, the recognition of its humanity, could be appreciated far beyond the borough of Brooklyn.

Sports have always been a laboratory for social issues. Robinson integrated big-league box scores eight years before the U.S. Supreme Court ordered the integration of public schools. Women's official debut in the Olympic Games, though limited to swimming, came in 1912, seven years before they got the right to vote. So even if these sports were late in opening their doors, in another way they were ahead of their time. And if it was necessary to break down some of those doors—Title IX support since 1972 for female college athletics comes to mind—so be it.

Another area of social importance, particularly as it affects young people, is substance abuse. High school, college, and professional teams are united in their opposition to the illegal use of drugs, tobacco, and alcohol. In most venues, testing is mandatory and tolerance is zero. Perhaps the most celebrated case occurred at the 1988 Olympic Games, when Canada's Ben Johnson surrendered his 100-meter gold medal after failing a drug test. Some athletes have lost their careers, and even their lives, to substance abuse. Other athletes have used their fame and success to caution young people about submitting to peer pressure and making poor choices.

Fans care about sports and sports personalities because they provide entertainment and identity. But they aren't the only ones who root, root, root for the home team. Government bodies come on board because sports spur local economies. When a city council votes to help underwrite the cost of a stadium or give financial advantages to the owners of a team, it affects the pocketbook of every taxpayer, not to mention the local ecosystem. When high schools and colleges allocate significant resources to athletics, administrators believe they are serving the greater good, but at what cost? These decisions are relevant far beyond the sports page.

In World War II, America's sporting passion inspired President Franklin Roosevelt to say professional games should not be cancelled. He felt the benefits to the national psyche outweighed the security risk of gathering huge crowds at central locations. In 2001, another generation of fans also continued to attend large-scale sports events because to do otherwise would "let the terrorists win." Being there, yelling your lungs out, cheering victory and bemoaning defeat, is a cleansing, even therapeutic exercise. The security check at the gate is just another price of stepping inside.

Unfortunately, there's a downside to all this. The notion that "Sports build character" is better expressed "Sports *reveal* character." We've witnessed too many coaches and athletes break the rules of fair play and good conduct, on and off the field. We've even seen violence and cheating in youth sports, often by parents of a (supposed) future superstar. We've watched fans "celebrate" championships with destructive behavior. I would argue, however, that these flaws are the exception, not the rule, that the good of sports outweighs the bad, that many of life's success stories took root on an athletic field.

Any serious examination of sports leads, inevitably, to the question of athletes as role models. Pro basketball star Charles Barkley created quite a stir in 1993 when he declared in a Nike shoe commercial, "I am not paid to be a role model." The knee-jerk response was, "But kids look up to you!" Barkley was right to raise the issue, though. He was saying that, in making lifestyle choices in language, clothing, and behavior, young people should look elsewhere for role models—ideally in their own home, to responsible parents.

The fact remains, however, that athletes occupy an exalted place in our society, at least when they are magnified in the mass media, and especially in the big-business, money-motivated sports. The athletes we venerate can be as young as a high school basketball player or as old as a Hall of Famer. (They can even be dead, as Babe Ruth's commercial longevity attests.) They are honored and coddled in a way few mortals are. We are quick—too quick—to excuse their excesses and ignore their indulgences. They influence the way we live (the food on our table, the cars in our driveway) and think (Ted Williams inspired patriotism as a fighter pilot during World War II and the Korean conflict; Muhammad Ali's opposition to the Vietnam War on religious grounds, validated by the Supreme Court, inspired the peace movement). No wonder we elect them—track stars, football coaches, baseball pitchers—to represent us in government. Meanwhile, television networks pay exorbitant sums to sports leagues so their teams can pay fortunes for players' services.

It has always been this way. If we, as a nation, love sports, then we, quite naturally, will love the men and women who play them best. In return, they give us entertainment, release, and inspiration. From the beginning of the 20th century until now, *Sports in America* is their story—and ours.

Larry Keith is a former writer and editor at Sports Illustrated. *He covered baseball and college basketball and edited the official Olympic programs in 1996, 2000 and 2002. He is a former adjunct professor of sports journalism at Columbia University and is a member of the Board of Visitors of the University of North Carolina School of Journalism.*

INTRODUCTION
1980–1989

IT WAS A DECADE OF EXCESS. IT WAS a time of a new "morning in America," as incoming President Ronald Reagan (1911-2004) called it after his election in 1980. Reagan served as President during some of the most financially prosperous years in American history.

The stock market soared. Peace symbols from the 1960s and 1970s were traded in for Mercedes-Benz logos, and tie-dyed T-shirts were replaced by three-piece suits. Business schools, investment banks and Wall Street law firms were filled with a new breed of achievers, called yuppies (young urban professionals), who were making money—and lots of it.

As the money poured in, many people succumbed to the lure of illegal drugs. Cocaine use soared, not just among the desperate poor, who were devastated by the scourge of crack-cocaine, but also among those well-off enough to afford the excess. The world of sports was by no means immune to either the draw of big money or the temptations of drugs— both mind-altering substances, such as cocaine, and performance-enhancing drugs, such as steroids.

There were several unfortunate examples of this. In 1986, college basketball superstar Len Bias, a young man destined for NBA stardom, died suddenly from cocaine use, just days after being drafted by the Boston Celtics. One of baseball's great pitchers, Dwight Gooden (b.1964) was suspended for cocaine use, just one year after leading the New York Mets to a World Series win in 1986 and just two years after a Cy Young Award-winning season. In and out of rehab for the next few years, the player known as "Doc" would never again be the pitcher he was. At the 1988 Summer Olympics in Seoul, South Korea, Canadian sprinter Ben Johnson was sent home in disgrace and stripped of his world-record gold medal after testing positive for performance-enhancing steroids.

The decade in sports began with a "miracle" (see page 10) and ended with a natural disaster (see page 86).

As American citizens were held hostage in Iran, the Soviet Union invaded Afghanistan and the cold war raged, a group of unknown college hockey players staged one of the greatest upsets in sports history, the so-called Miracle on Ice, at the 1980 Winter Olympic Games in Lake Placid, New York. It gave a boost to a nation that was burdened with double-

Morning in America   *Ronald Reagan is sworn in as President in January 1981 as his wife, Nancy, looks on.*

digit inflation, declining productivity and a diminished place on the world stage.

The decade drew to a shattering close as an earthquake struck San Francisco just moments before the start of game three of the 1989 World Series in Candle-stick Park. In an instant, players' chief concerns switched from the best game strategies to the safety of family members in the trembling stadium. Images of

1980–1989

players hugging their wives and carrying their children from the field reminded fans that no matter how important sports are—even the World Series—they are after all, just games. This was life—real, unstoppable and potentially deadly. The outcome of the Series seemed more an afterthought in the wake of this sobering reminder of the raw power of nature.

All three Summer Olympics in the 1980s were tainted by outside issues such as politics, boycotts and drug use. The line between sports and politics blurred as the United States boycotted the 1980 Summer Olympic Games in Moscow as a response to the Soviet Union's invasion of Afghanistan a year earlier. The Soviets returned the favor four years later, boycotting the 1984 Olympics in Los Angeles.

The role of business and money in sports had been growing decade by decade and reached new heights in the 1980s. Sneaker endorsements and multi-million dollar player contracts pushed the economics of sports to stratospheric levels, unthinkable a few years earlier. If baseball star Bobby Bonilla was worth $29 million, what would legendary heroes such as Mickey Mantle (1931–1995) or Ted Williams (1918–2002) be worth in the free-agent market had they been in their prime in the 1980s? If basketball player Moses Malone could be paid $13.2 million, what would 11-time champion Bill Russell (b.1934) or record-setting scorer Wilt Chamberlain (1936–1999) have been worth if they had been lucky enough to play in the 1980s?

Television money also gained a larger influence over sports. For the first time, most major sports team owners took in more money from selling television rights than from selling tickets to fans. As the money flowed in, players demanded that more of it flow into their pockets. Both baseball and football experienced prolonged player strikes as the battle for dollars supplanted the quest for victories.

Early in the decade, AIDS, a deadly new disease, emerged, at first believed to be limited to certain groups, but soon spreading to the wider population. Movie idol Rock Hudson's death from AIDS in 1985 put a familiar face on the previously shadowy disease, and placed its sadness

Happier Times *New York Mets pitcher Dwight Gooden (16) shares a laugh with Tom Seaver. Gooden was suspended for cocaine use one year after helping the Mets win the 1986 World Series.*

in the front of the American mind. A few years later, one of the 1980s' greatest athletes, Los Angeles Lakers basketball superstar Magic Johnson (b.1959), announced that he was HIV-positive (HIV is the virus that leads to AIDS).

But, as is always the case, the world of sports in the 1980s was not exclusively filled with bad news. The decade saw Wayne Gretzky (b.1961), a young hockey player from Brantford, Ontario, Canada, re-write the National Hockey League (NHL) record book on his way to becoming the greatest player of all time.

The National Basketball Association (NBA), which started the decade with its popularity at an all-time low, combined the play of Johnson and Larry Bird (b.1956) with the business and marketing brilliance of its new commissioner, David Stern (b.1942), to rocket its way to new heights of success. Along the way, the league's greatest rivalry (the Los Angeles Lakers and the Boston Celtics) was rekindled, and the Lakers won five titles.

Pete Rose (b.1941) became baseball's all-time hits leader, although by decade's end he was banned for life from the game he loved so much and played so well because of allegations that he had bet on baseball. Kareem Abdul-Jabbar (b.1947) became the NBA's all-time leading scorer, Walter Payton (1954–1999) became the leading rusher in the history of the National Football League (NFL), and Joan Benoit Samuelson (b.1957) proved that women could run Olympic marathons—in many cases faster than men.

The blending of sports and business was completed during the 1980s, and the

Court Battles *Magic Johnson (32) and the Los Angeles Lakers often went head-to-head with Larry Bird (right) and the Boston Celtics for the NBA title in the 1980s.*

intrusion of real-life issues such as drug abuse could not be kept from locker rooms. But from the glistening miracle in Lake Placid to the rumbling stands of Candlestick, many teams and individuals reminded us that despite the real world's rude intrusion into our beloved games, America's obsession with sports would only continue to grow.

1980

The Miracle on Ice

In theory, the Olympics are not supposed to be about politics. They provide an arena in which all countries can compete in the spirit of good sportsmanship, regardless of political viewpoints or outside conflicts.

In reality, the Olympics have always been politically charged: from African-American Jesse Owens' (1913–1980) one-man defeat of Adolf Hitler's "Aryan Olympics" in 1936, to the murder of Israeli athletes by terrorists in Munich, Germany, in 1972. But no Olympic decade was more politicized than the 1980s.

In 1980, the world's best athletes gathered in February in Lake Placid, New York, for the Winter Olympics. The Cold War between the United States and the Soviet Union was pretty hot, creating a special sense of rivalry between the athletes of the world's two superpowers.

The 1980 U.S. Olympic hockey team was made up of young college and minor league players who had never played together before the Olympic team was chosen. The national team from the Soviet Union was a powerhouse that had been playing together as a unit for many years.

That squad defeated the United States team 10–3 in an exhibition game a few weeks before the Olympics, and was considered by many experts to be the best hockey team in the world.

The stage was set for one of the greatest upsets in sports history. United States coach Herb Brooks knew his team didn't have as much raw talent as many of their opponents. Instead, he gave his team an intense sense of pride and the drive to succeed.

It worked. The American unit quickly became a team of destiny, playing before the home crowd in Lake Placid. They tied the talented team from Sweden in its opening game, then beat perennially powerful Czechoslovakia 7–3 en route to four wins and a tie in the opening round.

This qualified the Americans for the medal round, where they met the heavily-favored Soviets in the first game. The Soviet team had won the last four Olympic gold medals, and five of the last six. Their only defeat during this streak came in 1960, when they lost to the U.S. team, who took the gold medal at the games in Squaw Valley, California.

On February 22—which just happened to be George Washington's birth-

Miracles Do Happen *Jubilant U.S. hockey players celebrate their Olympic semifinal victory over the Soviet Union.*

day—the United States team faced off against the Soviet Union. The 10,000 fans at the Olympic Field House screamed and chanted "USA! USA!" as an electric atmosphere filled the building. Before the game, Brooks told his team, "You were born to be players. You were meant to be here. This moment is yours."

The Soviet Union jumped out to an early 1–0 lead. But the pesky, scrappy United States team tied it. The Soviets went back up 2–1, but as the clock ran down near the end of the first period, a rebound goal by American Mark Johnson tied the contest once again.

Hard checking by the American skaters and gutsy goaltending by United States goalie Jim Craig kept the game close. The Soviets never managed to extend their lead to more than one goal, and they left the ice at the end of the second period leading 3–2.

Johnson scored his second goal of the game—this one on a power play, while the Soviets were playing one man short—in the third period, tying the game and

1980

raising the decibel level of the crowd another notch. Halfway through the final period, United States captain Mike Eruzione found the net with a 30-foot slapshot that gave the Americans their first lead of the game.

Pandemonium broke loose in the crowd, and the chanting of "USA! USA!" continued non-stop. Now it was up to Craig and the United States' defense to hold the mighty Soviets scoreless.

Checking and swarming their opponents, the American team managed to prevent the Soviets from scoring. With the crowd counting down the final seconds, television broadcaster Al Michaels asked the millions of viewers across America his now classic question, "Do you believe in miracles?"

The United States team had done the impossible. They had beaten the best. Two days later, in the almost anticlimactic gold medal game, the United States beat Finland 4–2 to capture the gold. The outpouring of patriotism around the United States following the victory was as great as any since the end of World War II.

The Cold War dragged on for nine more years, and the political conflict between the United States and the Soviet Union affected the Olympics throughout the decade. But for one golden moment, the underdogs from the United States. had won a symbolic victory—and a well-earned gold medal.

Heiden's Golden Games

Over the course of nine days in February, American speed skater Eric Heiden (b.1958) did what no other Olympic athlete had ever done before at either the Winter or Summer Games—he won five individual gold medals in one Olympics. The 21-year-old speed skater from Madison, Wisconsin, dominated every event in which he participated.

Although at the time his astounding performance was somewhat overshadowed by the emotional victory of the United States hockey team, time has not diminished Heiden's accomplishment.

Heiden took part in five speed skating events, and won the gold medal in all five. He broke the Olympic record in winning the speed skating competitions at 500, 1,000, 1,500, 5,000, and 10,000 meters. He completed his gold-medal sweep—

Eric Heiden's 1980 Olympics Speed Skating Results

500 meters	38.03 seconds	Olympic Record	Gold Medal
1,000 meters	1 minute, 15.18 seconds	Olympic Record	Gold Medal
1,500 meters	1 minute, 55.44 seconds	Olympic Record	Gold Medal
5,000 meters	7 minutes, 02.29 seconds	Olympic Record	Gold Medal
10,000 meters	14 minutes, 28.13 seconds	World Record	Gold Medal

the drive for five, as it was called at the time—in the 10,000-meter race on February 23. Heiden had spent the previous day watching the United States upset the Soviets in hockey. Then he went out and smashed the existing world record in the 10,000 by more than six seconds.

"He gave the most dominant performance in the history of mankind in an Olympic competition," television announcer Keith Jackson said.

Boycott

Nowhere did the worlds of politics and sports clash more blatantly than in the United States' boycott of the 1980 Summer Olympic Games in Moscow. In December of 1979, the Soviet Union invaded neighboring Afghanistan, and U.S. President Jimmy Carter called for a boycott of the Games to protest the invasion.

On April 12, the United States Olympic Committee (USOC) voted to endorse Carter's call for a boycott. The vote was taken at a meeting in Colorado Springs attended by hundreds of athletes, plus sports and business leaders. Hours of angry debate followed, along with an appeal from Vice President Walter Mondale for everyone to support the boycott.

American athletes were devastated. They had trained for years, some had been preparing for the Games their entire lives and now, through no fault of their own, they would be denied the chance to compete at the Olympic level.

Twenty-five members of the 1980 United States Olympic team who were slated to go to Moscow sued the USOC. They claimed the USOC did not have the

Heiden— After the Gold Rush

Following the 1980 Winter Games, Eric Heiden avoided cashing in on his success. He did very few product endorsements, unlike fellow Olympic heroes Mark Spitz and Bruce Jenner. "Whenever I think of those guys, I don't like what they did," Heiden told ESPN. "They just sold themselves. It's like everyone owns a little piece of you."

Heiden retired from speed skating following his triumph in Lake Placid, but looked for a new athletic challenge. He found it in competitive bicycle racing, and immediately began training for the 1980 Summer Games.

He didn't qualify for the U.S. Summer Olympic team, but said that if he had, he would have defied President Jimmy Carter's (b.1924) boycott of the Games (see the story on this page). "Sports and politics don't mix," Heiden explained.

Heiden stuck with bicycle racing, winning the 1985 United States Pro Cycling Championship. A crash during the 1986 Tour de France led him to quit competitive cycling.

He enrolled in medical school and today is a practicing orthopedist in California.

power to decide not to enter an American team in the Olympics. They also claimed the law stated that any decision to not participate in an Olympic games had to be "sports-related." The court rejected all of their claims. The boycott stood.

More than 60 other countries joined the United States in the boycott and did not send teams to Moscow. Eighty-one countries did participate in the 1980 Moscow Games, including France, Great Britain, Italy, and Sweden.

It's Showtime!

In the spring of 1979, Earvin "Magic" Johnson's Michigan State University team beat Larry Bird's Indiana State

1980

University team for the National Collegiate Athletic Association (NCAA) basketball championship. That fall, both players entered the NBA as promising rookies for the 1979–80 season.

By the end of the 1980s, the rivalry between the two players dominated and re-defined professional basketball, bringing the NBA to new heights of popularity. Johnson's Los Angeles Lakers won five NBA championships during the decade, and Bird's Boston Celtics captured three NBA titles. The two teams met three times in the NBA Finals (1983–84, 1984–85 and 1986–87) during the Magic-Bird years.

Johnson's arrival in Los Angeles teamed him with center Kareem Abdul-Jabbar, creating a brand of basketball that came to be known as "Showtime."

At 6-foot-9, Johnson was the tallest point guard in NBA history. He ran the offense, scoring and passing. At a time in the league when individual performances dominated, Johnson got all his teammates involved in the offense, creating a true team effort.

Because of his height, speed and strength, Johnson could play forward or center, as well as guard. He demonstrated his versatility in game six of the NBA finals in 1980, when the Lakers met the Philadelphia 76ers on May 16.

Jabbar sprained his ankle in game five of the finals. The Lakers led the series three games to two, but they would have to play game six in Philadelphia without their all-star center.

Johnson, a rookie who had played all season at point guard, filled in for Jabbar at center. He scored 42 points, pulled down 15 rebounds, and dished out seven assists, leading the Lakers to a 123–107 victory to take the NBA title. Many consider it to be his finest game as a pro, stepping up when his team needed him most.

On thing was for certain: Showtime had arrived!

Borg Beats McEnroe at Wimbledon

In a match that lasted an astounding three hours and 53 minutes, 24-year-old Bjorn Borg (b.1956) of Sweden won his fifth consecutive Wimbledon singles tennis championship on July 5. His opponent in this titanic struggle was 21-year-old American John McEnroe (b.1959), who went on to win three of the next four Wimbledon singles titles.

Borg lost the first set 1–6, then came back to take the second 7–5. He grabbed the lead, winning the third set 6–3. The intense fourth set, which could have given Borg the title, ended with a marathon 34-point tiebreaker. McEnroe survived three match points and eventually won the tiebreaker 18–16, giving Borg a 6–7 defeat.

In the fifth and final set, Borg's serve overpowered McEnroe, giving the Swede 19 straight points and an 8–6 win. The victory represented Borg's fifth straight Wimbledon title and his 35th consecutive victory in a Wimbledon match—a tournament record.

Nicklaus Sets a Major Record

Jack Nicklaus (b.1940) is not only one of the greatest golfers of all time, but also one of the most consistent. From

1957 to 1998, Nicklaus played in a record 154 consecutive major championship tournaments for which he was eligible.

On August 10 Nicklaus won his record-setting 19th major tournament— far more than any other golfer in history— by capturing the PGA Championship at the Oak Hill Country Club in Rochester, New York. He shot a final round 69, taking the title by a record seven strokes.

The Golden Bear, as Nicklaus is known, finished with a 72-hole total of 274—six under par. The victory was his fifth in the Professional Golfers Association (PGA) Championship.

Holmes Spoils Ali's Bid for a Fourth Title

To many, he was always simply "the Champ," whether or not Muhammad Ali (b.1942) happened to own the heavyweight title at any given time. During the years when he was forbidden from boxing, he was called "The People's Champ." Millions around the world regarded him as a hero.

In 1960, Ali won the gold medal at the Olympics. In 1964, at the age of 22, he shocked the world by beating heavily favored Sonny Liston to capture the heavyweight championship. In 1967, when he refused to be drafted into the military because of his religious beliefs, the title was taken away from him. Then, in 1974, the 32-year-old Ali stunned the world again by beating the previously invincible George Foreman (b.1949) to capture the heavyweight title for a second time.

In 1978, Olympic gold medalist Leon Spinks beat Ali to take his title. Six months later, Ali won the rematch to grab the championship for a third time. After two years in retirement, the Champ tried for one more comeback.

On October 2, at the age of 38, Ali battled former sparring partner and current heavyweight champion Larry Holmes

Bear Market *Jack Nicklaus, the "Golden Bear," won more major golf championships than any other player in history. His 19th major title came at the PGA Championship in August.*

1980

(b.1949) in an attempt to capture the heavyweight title for a fourth time. Thirty-year-old Holmes danced and punched, showing the type of power and speed that were Ali's trademarks in his prime.

Ali was totally overmatched, moving slowly around the ring, taking non-stop punishment. When Ali failed to come out for the 11th round, Holmes was awarded the victory on a technical knockout. He retained his title.

Ali's fourth comeback attempt was over, and although he fought one more time, it became clear to his loyal legion of fans that his boxing career was finished. Holmes felt terrible about his victory, having just pummeled one of his own personal heroes. After the fight, Holmes went to Ali's hotel room to apologize.

Leonard Loses, Then Regains Welterweight Title

They could not have been more different in personality or boxing style. Welterweight champion Sugar Ray Leonard (b.1956) was a fast-moving, quick-legged dancer in the ring. He borrowed his boxing style and moves from Muhammad Ali and from his namesake, Sugar Ray Robinson, a welterweight and middleweight champion in the 1940s and

Other Milestones of 1980

✔ On January 26 in Philadelphia, Mary Decker became the first woman to run a mile in less than four and a half minutes. She was named the *Associated Press* Female Athlete of the Year for track.

✔ A total of 233 women competed in the Winter Olympic Games in Lake Placid, New York, compared to the 21 female athletes who competed there in the 1932 Games.

✔ On February 29, hockey great Gordie Howe (b.1928) scored his record 800th regular-season NHL goal, at the age of 51.

✔ Nineteen-year-old NHL rookie Wayne Gretzky won the first of his eight consecutive Most Valuable

Mary Decker

Player awards (also called the Hart Trophy). Gretzky became the youngest player ever to receive this honor.

✔ George Brett came closer to batting .400 than anyone else in Major League Baseball since Ted Williams did it in 1941. Brett stayed right near the .400 mark until late September, and ended the season with a .390 average.

✔ Grete Waitz of Norway beat her own course record with a time of 2:25:41 to win her third New York City Marathon in a row on October 26.

✔ The Women's Sports Foundation established the International Women's Sports Hall of Fame. Among its first inductees: tennis great Althea Gibson (b.1927).

1950s. Leonard's good looks and charming personality captured a legion of fans, and in many ways he filled the vacuum left by Ali's retirement.

"I studied Ali, I studied Sugar Ray Robinson, I watched them display showmanship, personality, and charisma," Leonard said in an interview on *ABC's Wide World of Sports*. "I wanted to transcend the sport. I wanted to be considered not just a fighter or a champion, but someone special."

Roberto Duran (b.1951), on the other hand, was a powerful puncher who destroyed opponents with his "hands of stone." Duran was already a great lightweight champion when he fought Leonard for the welterweight title, and he had much more experience. Their meeting on June 20, in Montreal, Canada, was perhaps the most eagerly anticipated non-heavyweight fight in history.

Duran was famous for his psychological intimidation. When he ran into Leonard on the street shortly before the fight, Duran made rude gestures, threats and insults to Leonard and his wife.

By the time the fight began, Leonard's trainer, Angelo Dundee—who had also trained Ali—recalled that Leonard was so angry at Duran about the insults that he was ready to go after him as if in a street brawl. Dundee reminded Leonard that his skills were superior and that he should outbox Duran, as they had planned.

But Leonard came out brawling, trying to beat Duran at his own game. After a 15-round slugfest, Duran won a unanimous decision, taking the welterweight title away from Leonard. A rematch was quickly scheduled.

In an interview with ABC Sports, Dundee explained Leonard's mindset going into the second fight. "He was embarrassed that he lost the first fight," Dundee said. "He realized what he was supposed to do the first time. And the first time, he was supposed to box. Ray was a premier boxer. What beats Duran, I knew, was a premier boxer."

In the rematch on November 25 at the New Orleans Superdome, Leonard stuck to the plan, outboxing and outdancing Duran for seven rounds, controlling the fight from the outset.

Then, in the eighth round, Duran threw up his hands and uttered the now-famous phrase, "No mas, no mas," which is Spanish for "No more." He quit the fight, claiming that he had stomach cramps, and Leonard regained his title.

Many at the fight said Duran appeared to lose heart, baffled by Leonard's shuffling feet and rapid-fire jabs. On that day, the skillful boxer beat the hands of stone.

1981

Wild Card Wins the Super Bowl

When the 1980–81 NFL season began, Oakland Raiders quarterback Jim Plunkett was on the bench, a spot with which he was quite familiar. Plunkett won the Heisman Trophy—college football's highest honor—in 1970. He joined Oakland in 1978, after NFL stints with the New England Patriots and San Francisco 49ers, but had been a rarely used backup during his first two years with the Raiders.

In the fifth game of the season, Raiders starting quarterback Dan Pastorini was injured. Plunkett took over and finished the season, leading Oakland to an 11–5 record and the wild-card spot in the playoffs. (The wild-card spot goes to the second-place team in the conference with the best record; that team gets to join the division winners in the playoffs.)

In the postseason, Plunkett led the Raiders to victories over the Houston Oilers, Cleveland Browns and San Diego Chargers, leading the team to its third Super Bowl. In the big game, on January 25, the Raiders met the Philadelphia Eagles, who were in their first Super Bowl.

Plunkett took control of the game right from the start. He threw three touchdown passes. The first was a two-yard toss to Cliff Branch in the first quarter. Then, just minutes later, Plunkett tossed a pass to running back Kenny King, which turned into an 80-yard score—the longest pass play in Super Bowl history. Plunkett's final touchdown pass was a 29-yarder to Branch in the third quarter.

Linebacker Rod Martin intercepted three Eagles' passes as the Oakland defense played tough, and the Raiders took the game 27–10.

Gretzky's Average Is Above Average

Wayne Gretzky's journey to re-write the NHL record books continued in his sophomore season, when Gretzky became the first player in the history of the league to average two points per game. His 1981 total was 164 points (goals plus assists) over an 82-game season. He had 55 goals and a record 109 assists.

These were just among the first of the mind-boggling statistics Gretzky posted during his NHL career. From the moment he set foot on the ice, he was the best

Strike Two *Baseball's second strike was the first to stop play in the middle of the season (see page 21).*

passer and the best scorer in NHL history. In 1981 he captured his second league MVP award, but the best was yet to come.

Thomas Leads Indiana to Victory

At the NCAA basketball championship game on March 20, the University of North Carolina jumped out to an 8–2 lead over University of Indiana, and later led by a score of 16–8. But Indiana's Randy Wittman helped close the gap, and his team led 27–26 at halftime.

As the game resumed in the second half, Indiana guard Isiah Thomas (b.1961) single-handedly put the contest away. During one seven-minute stretch at the beginning of the second half, the 6-foot-1 sophomore took over, leading Indiana to a 63–50 victory. He scored 10 of his game-high 23 points, consistently fed his teammates the ball, and pulled off key steals anytime it appeared that North Carolina was poised to get back into the game.

Earlier that same day, President Ronald Reagan was shot in an assassination attempt. It looked as if the game

1981

would be postponed. But when it became clear that the President was out of danger, the game proceeded. Still, a dark mood hung over the arena, dampening the usual frantic championship atmosphere.

The King of Daytona

Richard Petty's (b.1937) father, Lee Petty, began racing even before there was a National Association for Stock Car Automobile Racing (NASCAR, which began in 1949). And Richard slipped behind the wheel himself in 1958, beginning an unparalleled 34-year-career as a race car driver. His record 200 wins may never be surpassed, and his record of seven driving championships has been equaled only once (by the late, great Dale

Earnhardt). Petty's nickname, appropriately enough, was "the King."

The Daytona 500 is the biggest, most well-known stock car race of the season. In the first Daytona 500, in 1959, Richard Petty ran into engine trouble and had to leave the race. His father ended up winning that day. Richard won his first Daytona 500 race in 1964.

He opened the 1981 racing season with his record seventh and final victory at the Daytona 500 on February 15. He averaged 169.651 miles per hour in his Buick over the course of the race. Petty's seven victories at Daytona came in 1964, 1966, 1971, 1973, 1974, 1979, and 1981. Petty retired from racing in 1992.

Lewis Jumps to a Record

At the time, it was a huge achievement. Carl Lewis (b.1961), an extremely talented sophomore at the University of Houston, broke the world indoor long jump record in a meet on February 20. In retrospect, it was the first baby step for a man who would redefine the sport of track and field, picking up 10 medals in four Olympics—nine of those gold—over the next 16 years.

Lewis came into the Southwest Conference Indoor Track and Field Championship at Fort Worth, Texas, that February day as the NCAA champion in both the indoor and outdoor long jump.

The tall, 19-year-old from Birmingham, Alabama, broke the previous indoor record of 27 feet, 6 inches, set by Larry Myricks of Mississippi State in 1980. Lewis' personal best in the indoor long jump had been 27 feet, 4 inches. But this

The King *Richard Petty's trademarks included his hat, dark glasses, and engaging grin—plus a record 200 career NASCAR victories. Seven of those wins came at the prestigious Daytona 500.*

day he shattered both his own mark and the world record with a jump of 27 feet, 10.25 inches. To top off his record-breaking day, Lewis also won the 60-yard sprint, posting a time of 6.06 seconds—the third fastest time in history!

Strike Out!

Baseball, like all professional sports, is a diversion. For the fans, the games are a small break from the realities of life. But on June 12, the harsh reality of baseball as a business intruded, as the players went out on strike, stopping play and jeopardizing the season.

This was not the first baseball strike, nor would it be the last. On April 1, 1972, the first Major League Baseball strike in history began. Players walked out over a pension dispute. The strike was settled on April 13, and the season began on April 15, 10 days late.

As more players became free agents (that is, they had the right to negotiate with any team when their contract expired), salaries soared sky high. At the same time, television revenues grew increasingly more important in the financial structure of the game. Labor disputes between players and owners became what seemed like an annual event.

The 1981 strike was different. It was baseball's first midseason strike. Never before had the game been wrenched away from fans just as the pennant races were heating up. By the time it ended, the 1981 work stoppage was the longest strike in American sports history, shutting down the game for 50 days and wiping out more than a third of the season.

Carl Lewis:
The Best Ever

The 1984 Olympics were not supposed to be Carl Lewis' first, but the United States team boycotted the Games in 1980 (see page 13), so the track and field star had to wait four years. At the 1984 Games in Los Angeles, he won four gold medals. Some athletes might have stopped there, but for Lewis it was only the beginning.

He won gold medals in four Olympics (1984, 1988, 1992, and 1996), capturing 10 Olympic medals in all. Nine of them were gold, with the last medal coming at the age of 35 in Atlanta in 1996.

"He was the Babe Ruth and Michael Jordan of our sport," Pete Cava of the United States Track Federation told writer Michael Point.

"You always tried harder when Carl was competing," said American sprinter Leroy Burrell. "Part of it was the natural urge to win, but a lot of it was because you didn't want to get embarrassed."

Tom Tellez, Lewis' coach at the University of Houston, put it very simply: "He's the greatest athlete I've ever seen."

The main issue of the dispute was compensation for free agents. Today's baseball fan is used to seeing players leave their team when a contract is up to sign with a new team as a free agent—and the team they left receives nothing in return. But in 1981, the idea and practice of free agency was still very new. Owners felt that when a player left their team, some type of compensation was in order.

The players had fought for and won, at the bargaining table and in the courts, the right to become free agents without any compensation going back to the team they left. But the owners wanted to take back the players' victory, feeling they de-

1981

served something in return for players they lost to free agency.

To the players, this was totally unacceptable. After fighting for years to obtain free-agent status, they were not about to give up that hard-fought victory. And so the strike dragged on. Although they had called the strike, the players grew bitter,

blaming the owners for the lost baseball games. Older players grew frustrated as they tried to add to their career statistics. Younger players wanted to play a full season so they could continue developing their skills and establishing themselves.

And fans lost, perhaps most of all. For a baseball fan, the games are an inseparable part of the summer. Not being able to go to ballpark, or catch a game on television or radio, caused bitterness and anger toward both players and owners.

With the season approaching the point of cancellation, Marvin Miller, head of the Players' Association (the players' labor union), finally worked out a complex agreement that extended baseball's Basic Agreement, signed in 1980 between players and owners, without actually resolving the free-agent compensation issue.

All told, the strike caused the cancellation of 706 games (38 percent of the season), and cost the players $28 million and the owners $116 million. The owners, however, had taken out strike insurance, which made up for some of that loss.

The decision was made to turn 1981 into a split season—two separate seasons, really. The teams that were in first place in their respective divisions on June 11, when the last games were played, were declared winners of the first half of the season. A new "second season" began on August 10. All teams started with a 0-0 record. The teams that finished in first place over the second half of the season would meet the teams that won their divisions in the first half, in a best-of-five playoff series, adding an extra round to the postseason.

The games resumed, but it took awhile for fans to warm up to baseball

---

Baseball's Split Season

National League East

| FIRST HALF WINNER | Philadelphia Phillies |
| SECOND HALF WINNER | Montreal Expos |

Montreal beat Philadelphia three games to two in the East Divisional Series.

National League West

| FIRST HALF WINNER | Los Angeles Dodgers |
| SECOND HALF WINNER | Houston Astros |

Los Angeles beat Houston three games to two in the West Divisional Series.

National League Championship Series

Los Angeles beat Montreal three games to two .

American League East

| FIRST HALF WINNER | New York Yankees |
| SECOND HALF WINNER | Milwaukee Brewers |

New York beat Milwaukee three games to two in the East Divisional Series.

American League West

| FIRST HALF WINNER | Oakland Athletics |
| SECOND HALF WINNER | Kansas City Royals |

Oakland beat Houston three games to none in the West Divisional Series.

American League Championship Series

New York beat Oakland three games to none.

World Series

Los Angeles beat New York four games to two.

Other Milestones of 1981

✔ Mike Bossy of the New York Islanders became only the second player in NHL history to score 50 goals in the first 50 games of the season, tying Maurice ("the Rocket") Richard, who pulled off the feat in the 1944–45 season.

✔ On April 12, boxing great Joe Louis (1914–1981) died at age 66. Louis, who was known as the Brown Bomber, reigned as the heavyweight champion from 1937 to 1949.

✔ Jockey Bill Shoemaker won his record 8,000th race on May 27, far more than any other jockey in history.

✔ The longest game in baseball history was finally completed two months after it began. On April 18 the Pawtucket Red Sox and the Rochester Red Wings of the International League (a minor league) played 32 innings before the game was finally stopped at 4:07 the next morning. The game was completed on June 23, when Pawtucket scored in the 33rd inning for a 3–2 victory.

Nolan Ryan

✔ In a September 26 game against the Los Angeles Dodgers, Houston Astros pitcher Nolan Ryan (b.1947) threw his record breaking fifth no-hitter, surpassing Sandy Koufax's mark of four. Ryan eventually finished his baseball career with an astounding seven no-hitters.

✔ Pat Riley (b.1945) took over as coach of basketball's Los Angeles Lakers and led them to four more NBA titles in the 1980s. He took the team to the NBA Finals seven of the next eight seasons.

---

again. And the unusual split season set 1981 apart from all other baseball seasons in the record books. No team was hurt more by the split season than the Cincinnati Reds, who finished with the best overall record in baseball but didn't make the playoffs. They finished a close second in each half of the split season.

The Greatest Says Farewell

Simply put, he was "the Greatest." Three-time heavyweight champion Muhammad Ali was more than just a great athlete. At the height of the civil rights and anti-war movements in the 1960s, Ali was a symbol to millions around the world of standing up for what you believe in.

But by 1981, there was nothing left for the Champ to bring into the ring. After losing in his bid to regain the heavyweight title for a fourth time (see page 15) in a loss to Larry Holmes in 1980, Ali fought once more. On December 11, he lost a unanimous decision to Trevor Berbick.

Shortly after that fight, Ali announced his retirement from boxing. Then, not long after his retirement, Ali was diagnosed with Parkinson's Syndrome, brought on by the years of hits he took in the ring. With this sad and startling announcement, the world began to recognize the long-term effects of boxing.

1982

Playoff Marathon

The NFL postseason began with one of the most dramatic, exciting and memorable games in football history. On January 2, the San Diego Chargers met the Miami Dolphins in an American Football Conference divisional playoff game at the Orange Bowl in Miami. The game ended up pushing the physical, mental and emotional limits of the players, coaches and even the fans. It featured huge plays, blocked field goal attempts and an amazing comeback by the Dolphins.

San Diego jumped out to a 24–0 lead in the first quarter, and appeared to be unstoppable. They racked up the points on a 32-yard field goal by Rolf Benirschke, a 56-yard punt return by Wes Chandler, a one-yard touchdown run by Chuck Muncie and an eight-yard touchdown pass from quarterback Dan Fouts to running back James Brooks.

In the second quarter, Miami coach Don Shula replaced starting quarterback David Woodley with Don Strock. Strock brought Miami back into the game, engineering a long drive that resulted in a field goal, then tossing three touchdown passes to tie the game in the third period.

Fouts came right back with a 25-yard touchdown pass to Kellen Winslow, but Miami tied the score again when Strock connected with Bruce Hardy on a 50-yard touchdown pass. Early in the fourth quarter, Miami took its first lead of the game on a 12-yard touchdown run by Tony Nathan. Then, with 58 seconds left in the fourth quarter, Fouts forced an overtime period by finding James Brooks with a nine-yard touchdown pass to tie the game at 38–38. As time expired, Miami's Uwe von Schamann attempted a potential game-winning field goal, but it was blocked.

In overtime, where the first score meant victory, Schamann had another field-goal attempt blocked by the Chargers. San Diego's kicker, Rolf Benirschke, missed a field goal in the overtime period, as well.

Finally, after 13 minutes, 29 seconds of overtime play, Benirschke kicked a 29-yard field goal to give San Diego the victory by a score of 41–38.

Both quarterbacks were amazing and both teams played valiantly in a game that, unfortunately, someone had to lose. Fouts threw for 433 yards and three touchdowns, while Strock racked up 403 yards and four touchdowns.

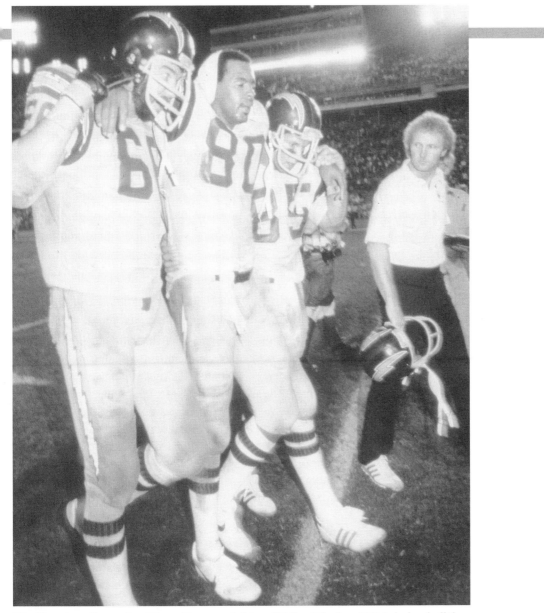

Working Overtime *San Diego Chargers tight end Kellen Winslow (80) is helped off the field by his teammates after a marathon NFL playoff victory over the Miami Dolphins.*

The game's most telling image, however, is the photograph of Chargers tight end Kellen Winslow being helped off the field by a pair of teammates after the conclusion of the contest (see above).

Winslow simply was exhausted after catching 13 passes and blocking a field goal in the muggy conditions. "Thank God it's over," he told his teammates. "It's the closest to death I've ever been."

1982

Montana Looks Super

There has never been a quarterback who operated with as much calm and grace in the most pressure-filled situations as Joe Montana (b.1956) of the San Francisco 49ers. It's almost as if he preferred to have the game or the season on the line with under a minute to go, 80 yards away from the winning touchdown. At the very least, he thrived on those high-pressure situations.

In January of 1982, Montana led the 49ers to their first Super Bowl appearance–and their first victory. By the time the decade ended, his would be a familiar face peering over center, coolly barking out signals, doing whatever needed to be done to bring victory in the biggest games.

The 49ers went on to win a total of four Super Bowls in the 1980s under Montana's leadership, clearly establishing themselves as the team of the decade. In his and the team's first Super Bowl, they faced another first-time entry, the Cincinnati Bengals, at the Pontiac Michigan Silverdome on January 24.

San Francisco was fresh off a dramatic 28–27 victory over the Dallas Cowboys in the NFC Championship Game. To pull that one out, Montana had tossed a six-yard touchdown pass to a leaping Dwight Clark in the back of the end zone with 51 seconds left in the game.

Although both teams were in the big game for the first time, Cincinnati really looked like the rookie squad, committing three turnovers in the first half, which the 49ers converted into 17 points en route to a 20–0 halftime edge. The first two turnovers—a Dwight Hicks interception

and a Lynn Thomas fumble recovery—occurred deep in the 49ers' own territory. Both led to long scoring drives.

In the second half, Cincinnati quarterback Ken Anderson brought the Bengals back to within six points, but a couple of San Francisco field goals sealed the 49ers' first Super Bowl victory. They took the game by a score of 26–21.

The championship marked a tremendous turnaround for Montana and the 49ers, led by coach Bill Walsh.

Walsh inherited a team that had been 2–14 in 1978 when he took over in 1979. The 49ers went 2–14 again that year, but were much improved offensively. Then, the season before their Super Bowl victory, the team finished with a 6–10 record. But in 1981, Walsh made Montana, a third-round draft pick in 1981, his full-time starting quarterback. Montana passed for 3,565 yards and 19 touchdowns, and the 49ers finished the regular season with a 13–3 record—the best in the league—which they followed up with their victory in the Silverdome.

The Shot

Although their future NBA battles would dominate the league in the 1990s, when Michael Jordan and Patrick Ewing (b.1962) faced off in the NCAA championship game on March 29, they were both just college freshman.

Ewing's Georgetown University team counted on the 7-foot-tall center's tough inside defense, rebounding and scoring. Jordan's University of North Carolina teammates looked to him to consistently hit his jump shots, racking up points.

Georgetown had a 32–31 lead at half-time. The second half featured fiercely competitive play, and neither team built up more than a four-point lead. Eric Smith and Sleepy Floyd added offense to Ewing's effort for Georgetown, while Jordan's jumpers and James Worthy's hard drives and defense kept North Carolina in the game.

Floyd gave Georgetown its last lead of the game when he hit a jump shot to put his team up 62–61 with 57 seconds left. North Carolina ran 25 seconds off the clock, then called a timeout to set up one final play.

Everyone in the building expected the play to go to Worthy, a junior and the team's leader. But North Carolina coach Dean Smith surprised Georgetown and showed great confidence in his freshman player by designing a play for Jordan.

With 15 seconds on the clock, Jordan did what he would come to do so many times during the years in which he dominated the NBA. He calmly hit a 16-foot jump shot, which proved to be the game winner.

Looking for the ball with the game on the line and coming through in the clutch became Jordan's professional trademarks, but he set the pattern way back in his freshman year at North Carolina, in the first of his many championship games.

The Great One

Some athletes redefine what people thought was possible in a sport. Before Babe Ruth came along in the 1920s, the idea of a baseball player hitting 60 home runs in a season sounded as likely

Air Apparent *Even in his college days, it was easy to see that Michael Jordan was a future NBA star. Jordan, shown here in a game against Wake Forest, helped deliver the NCAA title to North Carolina.*

as flying to the moon. In hockey, Wayne Gretzky rewrote the record books in the 1980s.

Gretzky scored an unheard-of 212 total points (goals plus assists) in the 1981–82 season, breaking his own NHL single-season record by 51 points.

In addition to his record for total points, Gretzky set a slew of other NHL single-season records: most goals (92), most assists (120), most hat tricks (three goals in a single game—he had 10), highest points-per-game average (2.65), and fastest to 50 goals (39 games).

1982

On his way to 212 points, Gretzky passed Phil Esposito's 76 goals in one season record, as well as his own assists record of 109. He scored five goals in one game, and four goals in a game three times. In an 82-game season, Gretzky was held scoreless only eight times. His team, the Edmonton Oilers, had the second best record in the NHL.

Gretzky, at the age of 21, won the MVP award, his third in three years.

Women Vie for Top NCAA Basketball Honors

In March 1982, the NCAA held its first women's championship basketball tournament. This was not, however, the first basketball championship for women. In 1972, the Association for Intercollegiate Athletics for Women (AIAW) held the first national women's college basketball tournament. At that time, the NCAA was not involved in women's sports. But by 1981, the NCAA began to stage a number of championships for women in tournaments that competed with the AIAW.

This year's tournament started with a 32-team field. Eventually, Louisiana Tech University beat Cheyney University of Pennsylvania by a score of 76–62 for the title. That first NCAA championship game drew 9,351 fans. The entire tournament

Born to Skate

Wayne Gretzky learned to skate at the age of two. Growing up in Brantford, Ontario, in Canada, young Gretzky learned the fundamentals of hockey from his father, Walter. By the age of six, he was already considered a prodigy, playing against 10-year-olds. At the age of eight, he scored 104 goals in a season, playing against 13-year-olds. At age 10 he scored 378 goals in 82 games.

When Gretzky reached the age of 15, he was already playing top level junior league hockey, always the youngest, yet always the best on his teams. He signed his first professional contract at age 17, playing for the World Hockey Association's Indianapolis Racers, who traded him to the WHA's Edmonton Oilers.

In 1979, the Oilers were accepted into the NHL and Gretzky began changing what was possible to achieve in hockey, setting new records each passing season.

Oilers coach Billy Harris said of Gretzky's 212-point 1981–82 season, "That's like rushing for 3,000 yards or hitting 80 home runs in a season."

It wasn't his overpowering physique that intimidated opponents. Gretzky was not particularly strong, nor fast, nor did he have a devastating slap shot. What he had was pure, uncanny instinct for the game, for seeing what was going to happen before it happened, for knowing where a teammate would be and getting a pass there, and for avoiding hard hits from the defense.

"Gretzky sees a picture out there that no one else sees," Boston Bruins executive Harry Sinden told ESPN. "It's difficult to describe, because I've never seen the game he's looking at."

brought in 56,320 people. Within a few years, that number had doubled, as women's college sports began to come into their own in the 1980s.

Before the NCAA got involved with women's college basketball, most of the best teams came from small, unknown colleges, like the two that made it to the finals that year. With the NCAA's involvement, many larger schools, which were better known for their men's basketball programs, began taking their women's athletic programs more seriously.

Watson's Day at the Beach

Tom Watson beat Jack Nicklaus in a dramatic head-to-head duel in the fourth and final round of golf's U.S. Open in June at Pebble Beach, California. Watson won by making one of the most memorable shots in golf history.

After 16 holes of the last round, Watson and Nicklaus were tied atop the leaderboard. Then, on the par-three 17th, Watson's tee shot landed beyond the green in heavy, treacherous rough. He was only about 15 feet from the hole, but a delicate pitch shot could have cost him the tournament if not executed properly—too short, and he's still in the rough; too long, and he could bogey the hole. "Get it close," Watson's caddy told him. "No, I'm going to make it," Watson replied.

And he did. As Watson's pitch trickled into the cup, he danced around the green in joy. Watson went on to birdie the 18th hole also to win by two shots.

The next month, Watson completed a rare feat when he followed his U.S. Open triumph by winning the British Open.

We're Number One! *Forward Ann Pendergrass and her Louisiana Tech teammates won the first NCAA women's basketball championship by beating Cheyney University in the final game.*

The Specter of Drugs

More and more as the decades of the 20th century unfolded, sports came to reflect what was happening in the rest of American society. As drug use increased, the dark specter of substance abuse raised its terrifying head in the world of sports.

How much was known of cocaine use in the NFL in the 1980s is hard to say. Did players hide it from each other? From

1982

coaches? From team officials? Or was there an unspoken "look the other way" policy?

When the July 14 issue of *Sports Illustrated* magazine hit the newsstands in 1982, a bright light was shed on this dark secret. Don Reese, a retired defensive end who had played for the Miami Dolphins (1974–76), the New Orleans Saints (1978–80) and the San Diego Chargers (1981), told the magazine that cocaine "now controls and corrupts" NFL football, because so many players in the league used it.

Reese himself was sentenced in 1977 to one year in prison for selling cocaine. He called the problem a growing cancer in the league. "Cocaine can be found in quantity throughout the NFL," Reese said in the article, which he co-wrote with *Sports Illustrated* staff writer John Underwood. "It's pushed on players, often from the edge of the practice field. Sometimes it's pushed by players. Prominent players. A cocaine cloud covers the entire league. I think most coaches know this or have a good idea."

Reese told of his own drug use, which included free-basing (inhaling cocaine in a smokable form) with several other members of the Saints. At the time of the article, Reese still owed $30,000 to drug dealers and said he had been threatened by these dealers several times.

In 1980, the NFL had introduced a voluntary program to enable players with drug and alcohol problems to find help. As of 1982, 17 players had taken advantage of the program. As cocaine use spiraled out of control in America during the 1980s, its effect on sports grew as well, and could no longer be ignored.

Decker Sets Another Record

Mary Decker already owned the world record for the fastest time in the women's 5,000-meter race, the 3,000-meter race, the 2,000-meter race, and the 800-meter race when she took off in the 10,000-meters at Hayward Field in her hometown of Eugene, Oregon, on July 16.

One week earlier at an international meet in Paris, Decker set a new women's world record in the mile, turning in a time of four minutes, 18.08 seconds. Now, with the hometown crowd cheering her on, she set a world record in the 10,000, finishing in 31 minutes, 35.30 seconds. The 10,000-meter race had been dominated by Soviet women, who held the nine fastest times in the event, before Decker's world-record run.

As "Little Mary Decker" (she was only 4-foot-10, 86 pounds), she burst onto the international track and field scene in 1973 at a United States-Soviet meet in Minsk. Her breakthrough year was 1980, when she set three world records. Later, she went on to win the 1,500- and 3,000-meter races at the 1983 World Championships in Helsinki, Finland.

But 1982 was the finest year of her career, when she set records in the 2,000-, 3,000-, 5,000-, and 10,000-meter races, as well as her triumph in the mile. For her achievements, Decker was voted the Women's Sports Foundation's Amateur Sportswoman of the Year. She also won the Jesse Owens Award, which is presented annually to the best U.S. track and field athlete. She became the first woman to win that prestigious award.

King of Steals

The Oakland Athletics' Rickey Henderson (b.1958)—baseball's all-time stolen base leader and the man considered by many to be the greatest leadoff hitter the game has ever seen—broke the single-season stolen base record on August 27 in a game at Milwaukee against the Brewers.

Henderson broke the record that had been set by St. Louis Cardinals' great Lou Brock, who stole 118 bases in 1974. Henderson stole base number 119 in the third inning, after drawing a walk from Brewers pitcher Doc Medich. Medich tossed over to first four times to chase Henderson back to the bag. He then threw a pitchout to catcher Ted Simmons as Henderson started for second.

The throw by Simmons to Brewers shortstop Robin Yount was a good one, but as he had done so many times, even against perfect throws, Henderson slid in under the tag and was safe at second.

The game was stopped and members of both teams and the media gathered around Henderson at second base. The Oakland speedster pulled the base from the ground and held it over his head triumphantly. Among the crowd was American League President Lee MacPhail and Brock himself, who offered congratulations on the breaking of his record.

Henderson went on to steal three more bases in that game, and finished the season with a total of 130, still the modern single-season record. He eventually played through the 2003 season, and ended his 25-year career with 1,406 thefts, another record.

NFL Strike Becomes the Longest

For the first time in NFL history, players staged a strike that interrupted the regular-season schedule. The strike began on September 21, two games into the 1982 season. By the time it ended 57 days later, on November 16, it had become the longest strike in professional sports history, surpassing the baseball strike of 1981 by seven days. (The baseball strike of 1994, which led to the cancellation of the playoffs and World Series, is the current record holder. It lasted 234 days.)

As with the 1981 baseball strike, the issue was money. And once again, as would happen more and more frequently in the 1980s and beyond, fans turning to the sports page would come to read about labor negotiations, team revenues and player salaries, instead of games won and lost. Sports was business, and the business of

Top Basestealing Seasons of the 20th Century

PLAYER	TEAM	SEASON	STOLEN BASES
Rickey Henderson	Oakland Athletics	1982	130
Lou Brock	St. Louis Cardinals	1974	118
Vince Coleman	St. Louis Cardinals	1985	110
Vince Coleman	St. Louis Cardinals	1987	109
Rickey Henderson	Oakland Athletics	1983	108
Vince Coleman	St. Louis Cardinals	1986	107
Maury Wills	Los Angeles Dodgers	1962	104
Rickey Henderson	Oakland Athletics	1980	100
Ron Leflore	Montreal Expos	1980	97
Ty Cobb	Detroit Tigers	1915	96

Other Milestones of 1982

✔ Carl Lewis broke the 28-foot mark in the long jump in January, setting a new world record. He leapt a distance of 28 feet, 1 inch, in the United States Olympic Invitational track meet.

✔ On January 26, Cheryl Miller, future NCAA basketball great, scored 105 points in a high school game for Riverside Polytechnic in California.

✔ Relief pitcher Rollie Fingers of the Milwaukee Brewers became the first baseball pitcher in history to rack up 300 career saves.

✔ Martina Navratilova (b.1956) began her incredible run in women's tennis by winning 90 of 93 matches.

Shirley Muldowney

✔ Sugar Ray Leonard retired from boxing due to an eye injury. His record was 32–1, with 22 knockouts. His only loss came at the hands of Roberto Duran (see page 16).

✔ Lorri Bauman of the Drake University Bulldogs scored 50 points in a West Regional basketball game against the University of Maryland. Although Maryland won that game 89–78 to advance to the Final Four, Bauman's total still stands as the most points ever scored in an NCAA women's tournament game.

✔ Steve Carlton of the Philadelphia Phillies, who won 23 games at age 37, became the first pitcher to win four Cy Young Awards.

✔ Shirley Muldowney won her third National Hot Rod Association points title—the only driver, male or female, to ever win three.

✔ Kathy Whitworth was inducted into the World Golf Hall of Fame. Her 88 career victories are the most by an American.

✔ The Supreme Court ruled that Title IX covers coaches and other school employees as well as students. Title IX is a federal regulation that mandates equal funding for boys' and girls' programs, including athletic programs, at schools in the United States.

✔ Tear-away jerseys appeared for the first time in college football. A tear-away jersey easily tears off when grabbed by an opposing player, so that the wearer can't be pulled down by his jersey.

sports had grown so big by the 1980s that at times the games seemed secondary to financial deals and labor disputes.

One major issue in this strike was the fact that before 1982 the NFL Players Association (the players' labor union) was not allowed to receive copies of players' contracts. Each player had no idea how much anyone else was making. In some cases, backup players were making more than the starters they were supposed to cover for. After the strike, contracts and salaries were a more open issue, as the union was allowed to receive all contract information. Minimum salaries were established, and free-agency was expanded.

When the strike was finally settled, the decision was made to reduce the number of games in the 1982 season to nine—the two played before the strike, plus seven more after. In addition, 16 teams qualified for the playoffs (six more than usual), and the regular season ended a week later than originally scheduled.

The strike cost the league $240 million in lost ticket and television money, and wiped 112 games from the schedule. The resulting agreement was set to last until 1986 and brought the players $60 million in bonuses, plus $1.3 billion in salaries and benefits for the years 1983–86.

Attendance for the games played after the strike was down greatly, and it took almost a full year for fans to return to the NFL in pre-strike numbers.

Bye-Bye Oakland

Colorful and controversial Oakland Raiders owner Al Davis wanted to move his team from Oakland to Los Angeles. The NFL said no. As was becoming the case more and more often in sports in the 1980s, the two sides ended up in court.

Davis sued, claiming an antitrust violation, saying the league had no right to tell him where he could or couldn't move his team. Following a long and bitter court battle, a jury awarded Davis the right to move his team to Los Angeles.

And so, before the 1982 season, Davis moved his Raiders about 500 miles south. The team began playing its home games in the Los Angeles Coliseum instead of the Oakland Coliseum. (The franchise eventually reversed course in 1995 and went back up north to Oakland, where it remains...for now.)

The ruling shook up the NFL, which saw moves by the Cleveland Browns, Los Angeles Rams and Houston Oilers in the years that followed this momentous decision. And once again, the sports pages were filled with stories of owners, lawyers, judges and juries to accompany those about athletes.

1983

Riggins' Run

The NFL's longest postseason climaxed with one of the most memorable runs in league history. John Riggins, the Washington Redskins' burly fullback, raced 43 yards for the go-ahead touchdown in the fourth quarter of his team's 27–17 victory over the Miami Dolphins in Super Bowl XVII at Pasadena, California on January 30.

The strike-shortened regular season (see page 31) resulted in a 16-team postseason tournament in which Riggins was the unquestioned star. He carried the Redskins by rushing more than 100 yards in each of their three NFC playoffs wins, then had 166 yards in the Super Bowl.

Washington trailed Miami 17–13 until Riggins' decisive run came on a fourth-down-and-1 play with 10:01 remaining in the game.

New Football League Signs Heisman Winner

The United States Football League (USFL) began play in 1983. Playing a 16-game schedule in the spring, so as not to go head-to-head with the NFL's fall season, the new league featured colorful owners, such as New York real estate magnate Donald Trump, and competed with the NFL for top college players.

Founded by David Dixon, a New Orleans art and antiques dealer, the USFL announced its formation on May 11, 1982. Judge Peter Spivak, part owner of the Detroit team, was the president of the league. Eventually, Chet Simmons, a broadcasting executive with ESPN, was named the league's first commissioner.

The USFL started with 12 teams in major markets across the country: New Jersey, Los Angeles, Chicago, Detroit, Boston, Tampa, Oakland, Denver, Washington, Philadelphia, Birmingham and San Diego (that franchise moved to Phoenix). The games were shown on ESPN and ABC.

Shortly before the start of their inaugural season, the New Jersey Generals signed University of Georgia tailback Herschel Walker, 1982's Heisman Trophy winner (the Heisman Trophy is awarded annually to the best college football player in the nation).

Walker left college a year early to turn pro, and the highly touted rookie gave instant credibility to the new league.

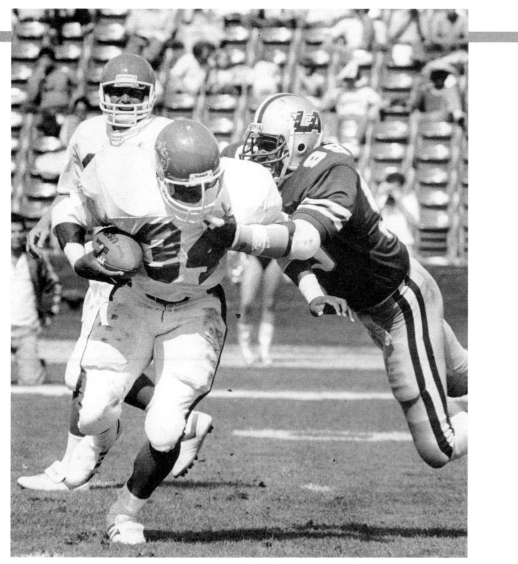

Instant Exposure *Running back Herschel Walker (34) made headlines when he joined the USFL; the new football league played in front of a lot of empty seats, however.*

During his college career, Walker rushed for 5,259 yards and set 10 NCAA records.

Walker's contract with New Jersey made him the highest paid player in football history. He received $1.5 million, compared to Chicago Bears running back Walter Payton, who had the top NFL salary of $700,000.

Although USFL's level of play was not up to NFL quality, the teams averaged more than 24,000 fans a game, which was about what they had hoped for. The ratings were also good. But huge player salaries put many teams into financial trouble—trouble that would plague the USFL throughout its entire existence.

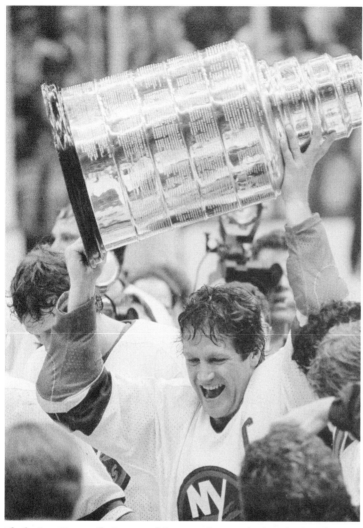

Their Cup Runneth Over and Over and. . . *Winning the Stanley Cup championship was getting to be old hat for captain Dennis Potvin and the New York Islanders, who won their fourth straight NHL title.*

Islanders Win Fourth Straight Stanley Cup

Since the formation of the NHL in 1917, no team has dominated the league the way the Montreal Canadiens have. In hockey, the word "dynasty" usually means Montreal. The Canadiens have won the Stanley Cup championship 23 times since then (that's by far a league record; the next closest, the Toronto Maple Leafs, stand at just 13 championships). Between 1955 and 1960 the Canadiens won five consecutive Stanley Cups, a feat that has never been equaled. Then, from 1975 to 1979, the Canadiens won four straight Stanley Cups.

In 1983, the New York Islanders became just the second team in NHL history to win four Stanley Cups in a row, creating their own dynasty and joining Montreal in the record books.

The streak began with a Stanley Cup Championship in the 1979–80 season, when the Islanders beat the Philadelphia Flyers in six games in the finals. In 1980–81, the Isles (as their fans call them) beat the Minnesota North Stars in five games in the finals. The 1981–82 finals saw the Islanders sweep the Vancouver Canucks in four straight games.

New York took its fourth straight Cup in May, completing another four-game sweep in the 1982–83 finals by beating the Edmonton Oilers, who were led by the Great One, Wayne Gretzky. During the regular season, Gretzky scored 71 goals and had 196 points on the way to his fourth straight MVP award. But in the Stanley Cup finals, the Islanders tough defense shut down Gretzky and his Oilers' teammates.

The Oilers were held to just six goals in the four-game series, and they didn't score off Islanders goaltender Billy Smith in seven of the 12 periods played. Islanders Bryan Trottier and Butch Goring stuck close to Gretzky, limiting him to just four assists. The Islanders' offense was led by Mike Bossy and Clark Gillies.

Tom Watson Wins Fifth British Open

American golfer Tom Watson won his fifth British Open golf championship in July. This achievement is unique in recent times, and places Watson second only to Harry Vardon, who won six British Opens between the years 1896 and 1914.

Watson took the Open with a combined four-round total of 275 at the Royal Birkdale course in England. His other victories in the British Open came in 1975, 1977, 1980 and 1982.

Watson joined the PGA Tour in 1971, and was the leading money winner on the Tour in 1977, 1978, 1979, 1980 and 1984. He was voted PGA Player of the Year six times (1977, 1978, 1979, 1980, 1982 and 1984), and was a member of four United States Ryder Cup teams (1977, 1981, 1983 and 1989). He served as captain in 1993.

Watson also won the Vardon Trophy (named for Harry Vardon) three years in a row (1977–79). The Vardon Trophy is awarded by the PGA of America to the PGA Tour regular with the lowest average score for the year.

Malone Leads 76ers to NBA Championship

In these days of high-priced free agents, it doesn't seem unusual for a pro team to go out and spend millions to land the player they need. But in the 1980s, the concept was still new.

The Philadelphia 76ers had not won an NBA title since 1967. Team owner Harold Katz decided to go out and buy a top star to team with Julius Erving, the 76ers' perennial All-Star, for the 1982–83 season.

The man he turned to was 6-foot-10 center Moses Malone. Malone had been the first player to go straight from high school into pro basketball, without going to college. Like Erving, Malone began his pro career in the American Basketball Association (ABA), a rival league that eventually merged several of its teams into the NBA.

From 1974 to 1976, Malone was a dominant center, a powerful rebounder, and a prolific scorer for the ABA's Utah Stars and St. Louis Spirit. When the two leagues merged in 1976, Malone joined the Buffalo Braves, then later played for the Houston Rockets, where he continued to be among the league leaders in scoring and rebounding. Following the 1981–82 season, he became a free agent, which is when Katz and the 76ers came calling.

Determined to bring a championship home to the loyal fans in Philadelphia, Katz gave Malone a contract worth $13.2 million over four years, an unheard-of figure in the NBA at that time. But it paid off. During the regular season, Malone averaged 24.5 points per game, and a league-leading 15.3 rebounds per game. Those numbers only improved during the playoffs, when Malone kicked his game into a higher gear, averaging 25.8 points and 18.5 rebounds per game.

Led by Malone at center and Erving at forward, the 76ers compiled a devastating 12–1 playoff record en route to the title, including a four-game sweep of the Los Angeles Lakers in the NBA Finals. In the decisive game, on May 31 in Los

Angeles, Malone scored 24 points and pulled down 23 rebounds to beat Magic Johnson and the defending champion Lakers 115–108.

Who said that you cannot buy a championship?

The Pine Tar Incident

It was surely one of baseball's strangest and most controversial moments. On July 24, the Kansas City Royals were at Yankee Stadium, playing just another regular-season game against the Bronx Bombers. With two outs and nobody on base in the top of the ninth inning, the Yankees led 4–3. The Royals' U.L. Washington hit a single, bringing up Kansas City third baseman George Brett.

Brett smashed a two-run homer off Yankees relief pitcher Goose Gossage, giving the Royals a 5–4 lead. Or so everyone in the stadium thought.

Once Brett crossed home plate and had gone into the Kansas City dugout,

however, Yankees manager Billy Martin walked up to home plate umpire Tim McClelland and handed him Brett's bat, complaining that the bat was illegal because it had too much pine tar.

Pine tar is a dark, sticky substance that players put onto their bat handles to get a better grip. While use of the pine tar is legal, the amount a player may use is specified in the rules. A player may not place any substance on his bat to improve the grip that extends more than 18 inches from the end of the bat handle.

The umpires all met around home plate, measuring the amount of pine tar on the bat against the front side of home plate (which they knew to be 17 inches long). The umpires ruled that there was more than 18 inches of pine tar on the bat, and so McClelland signaled that Brett was out and the home run did not count.

The Royals' third baseman sprang from the dugout, racing toward McClelland, his eyes bulging with rage, a stream of obscenities pouring from his lips. Umpiring crew chief Joe Brinkman intercepted Brett before he reached McClelland, grabbing him around the neck and trying to calm him down. Royals manager Dick Howser and coach Rocky Colavito joined the fray, and were soon ejected from the game along with Brett.

Meanwhile, Brett's Kansas City teammate, future Hall-of-Fame pitcher Gaylord Perry, slipped out of the dugout, grabbed the bat, and headed for the clubhouse to hide it. Perry was stopped by stadium security, who took the bat back and ejected Perry from the stadium.

The home run was nullified, and the Yankees won the game 4–3. Or so every-

---

The Pine-Tar Rule

Rule 1.10 (c) of the official baseball rulebook states:

> The bat handle, for not more than 18 inches from its end, may be covered or treated with any material or substance to improve the grip. Any such material or substance, which extends past the 18-inch limitation, shall cause the bat to be removed from the game.

Following the George Brett pine-tar incident, this rule was amended to read:

> NOTE: If the umpire discovers that the bat does not conform to (c) above until a time during or after which the bat has been used in play, it shall not be grounds for declaring the batter out, or ejected from the game.

---

one at the stadium thought. But the Royals protested the decision, arguing that there was no intentional plan to cheat and that they did not violate the spirit of the rules. American League president Lee MacPhail agreed. He overruled the umpires' decision, stating that the game should resume from the point at which the pine-tar incident occurred—in other words, after Brett's home run, which would now count, and give the Royals a 5–4 lead.

Twenty-five days after it began, on August 18 (an open date for both teams), the "pine-tar game" resumed at Yankee Stadium in front of only 1,245 fans. Kansas City's Hal McRae made the final out in the top of the ninth inning, then Royals pitcher Dan Quisenberry set the Yankees down 1-2-3 in the bottom of the ninth inning to give Kansas City the victory.

Following this incident, baseball's rule book was amended to prevent a similar situation from occurring again (see the box on the opposite page).

When Brett was elected to the Baseball Hall of Fame in 1999, the famous pine tar bat went to Cooperstown with him, where it was placed on display.

Navratilova's First U.S. Open

Continuing her meteoric rise to the top of women's tennis, Martina Navratilova defeated Chris Evert-Lloyd on September 10 to capture her first U.S. Open singles championship. In a match that lasted only 63 minutes, Navratilova crushed Evert-Lloyd 6–1, 6–3. Cementing her stature as the top women's tennis

On Top of the World *Martina Navratilova left no doubt that she was the best women's tennis player in the world with an easy, straight-sets victory over Chris Evert in the finals of the U.S. Open.*

player in the world, Navratilova dominated her opponent, top rival, and friend, rushing the net after nearly every serve, keeping Evert-Lloyd from setting up on the baseline or ever truly getting settled and comfortable.

1983

The victory was Navratilova's 66th in her last 67 matches. By the end of 1983 she posted a record of 86–1, to follow the 90–3 record she put up in 1982. The former Czech defector (now an American) added the victory on the U.S. Open's hard, fast surface to her earlier wins on the grass courts of Wimbledon, England, and on the clay courts at Hilton Head, South Carolina.

Navratilova continued to dominate women's tennis throughout the 1980s with an aggressive and intimidating style that changed the face of the game (see box).

Three Royals Head to Jail

For the first time, three active Major League Baseball players were arrested and sent to jail on drug-related charges. On November 17, a federal judge sentenced Willie Wilson, Willie Aikens, and Jerry Martin of the Kansas City Royals to three-month jail sentences for attempting to purchase cocaine. All three had pleaded guilty.

Noting the special place in society he felt professional athletes held, the judge also fined Wilson and Aikens the

The Changing Face of Women's Tennis

Martina Navratilova's great contributions to the game of tennis can't be limited to her astounding 56 Grand Slam titles. (The Grand Slam is made up of tennis' four major tournaments: the Australian Open, the French Open, Wimbledon, and the U.S. Open.) She also took women's tennis to a new level of excitement and fan interest in the 1980s, bringing speed, power, and strength to the game. Navratilova introduced new training methods and nutritional programs specifically designed for female tennis players.

At age four, in her native Czechoslovakia, Navratilova got her first tennis racquet. At age six, she took her first lesson. When she was eight, she entered her first tournament. By the age of 16, she had become Czechoslovakia's top player.

In 1975, Navratilova defected to the United States, and by the mid-1980s she was well on her way to set-

ting new standards for women's tennis. She changed the look and style of the women's game, making it faster and more athletic. After winning six Wimbledon titles in a row, from 1982 to 1987, to bring her total to eight, Navratilova returned to the finals in 1990 for her record-breaking ninth Wimbledon victory.

Her success inspired many girls, not only to become tennis players, but also to take part in athletics of many kinds. She had another impact off the court as well, beginning in 1981, when it became widely known, and she confirmed in interviews, that she was gay. Few athletes of her caliber have ever "come out of the closet," and she faced some criticism for her lifestyle. However, she battled against those opinions with the same power that she used to win on the court, and became an important spokesperson for the cause of fair treatment for gay and lesbian athletes.

Other Milestones of 1983

✔ Paul (Bear) Bryant (1913–1983), the winningest coach in college football history at the time (with 323 victories), died on January 26 at the age of 69.

✔ San Diego Padres first baseman Steve Garvey played in his 1,118th consecutive baseball game on April 16, setting a new National League record.

✔ On May 31, Jack Dempsey (1895–1983), heavyweight boxing champ from 1919 to 1926, died at age 87.

✔ Rap music picked up sports culture as a theme when Grandmaster Flash released "The Message," in which he talked about "watching the game or the Sugar Ray fight." Also, rapper Kurtis Blow released the song "Basketball," a tribute to the NBA players he watched in the 1970s.

Evelyn Ashford

✔ Evelyn Ashford (b.1957) set a world record for women in the 100-meter run with a time of 10.79 seconds on July 3 at the National Sports Festival in Colorado Springs.

✔ Philadelphia Phillies pitcher Steve Carlton picked up his 300th career victory on September 23. Carlton struck out 12 batters in eight innings and beat the St. Louis Cardinals 6–2 to record his milestone win.

✔ NFL pioneer and longtime Chicago Bears coach George Halas (1895–1983) died on October 31 at age 88.

✔ Overtime for regular-season NHL games was reinstated for the first time since 1942, with a five-minute time limit. Before then, games simply ended in a tie.

maximum amount of $5,000, and he fined Martin $2,500. Martin and Aikens were released by the Royals. Wilson, the team's starting centerfielder, remained with the organization.

Commissioner Bowie Kuhn also suspended the players from baseball for one year, as the growing problem of illegal drug use among professional athletes leapt once again to the front page.

1984

Olympic Gold on the Ski Slopes

Lightning did not strike twice. After its "Miracle on Ice" victory at the 1980 Winter Olympics (see page 10), the U.S. hockey team failed to qualify for the medal round at the 1984 Winter Games in Sarajevo, Yugoslavia.

However, going into the Winter Games, the United States had never won a gold medal in Olympic downhill skiing. That changed on the slopes of Sarajevo. Before the competition ended, the U.S. ski team took gold medals in three of the six downhill events—competition that had traditionally been dominated by European skiers.

The first gold medal ever won by the United States in the downhill was captured on February 16 by a colorful 23-year-old from California named Bill Johnson. He tore down the 3,066-meter course in one minute, 45.59 seconds, beating Peter Mueller of Switzerland by 27-hundredths of a second. Johnson, who trailed for most of the run, caught up to and passed Mueller's time with a powerful burst of speed just before he crossed the finish line.

American brothers Phil and Steve Mahre followed Johnson's performance with gold and silver medal victories in the men's Alpine slalom. Phil took the second U.S. downhill gold with a time of one minute, 39.41 seconds, while Steve won the silver.

Not to be outdone, the American women's downhill team also pulled off a one-two finish. That came in the giant slalom, with Debbie Armstrong capturing the third U.S. downhill gold of the games with a time of two minutes, 20.98 seconds. American Christin Cooper took the silver.

The other notable performance by an American at the Sarajevo Games came from men's figure skater Scott Hamilton, who captured the gold in the men's individual competition. Hamilton became the first American to do so in 24 years.

Kareem Passes Wilt

There have been a handful of centers in the history of the NBA whose play was so dominant, whose sheer physical ability was so superior, that they changed the way the game is played. Teams had to adjust their strategies to

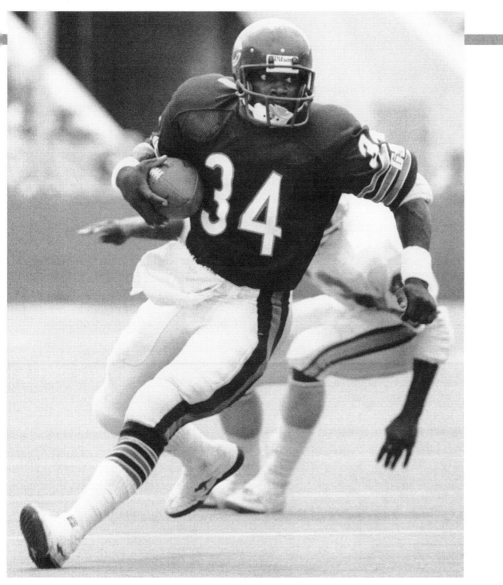

Payton's Place   *Chicago Bears running back Walter Payton ascended to the top of the NFL's all-time rushing chart in a game in October (see page 45).*

stop these players from scoring, rebounding or controlling the game on the defensive end of the court.

George Mikan of the Minneapolis Lakers was the first of this breed in the early days of the NBA. Bill Russell of the Boston Celtics helped his team build a championship dynasty in the 1950 and 1960s with his powerful shot blocking, rebounding and defense. Today, Shaquille O'Neal of the Los Angeles Lakers fits the role of the dominant center who can single-handedly change the balance of any basketball game.

1984

Among this elite group, two centers, both of whom began their pro careers elsewhere but eventually came to glory with the Lakers, rose above the rest offensively—Wilt Chamberlain in the 1960s and Kareem Abdul-Jabbar in the 1980s.

On April 5, Abdul-Jabbar hit his trademark skyhook—a high, arcing shot—with eight minutes, 53 seconds remaining in a game against the Utah Jazz. That brought his career scoring total to 31,421 points to surpass Chamberlain as the NBA's all-time leading scorer. (Chamberlain, who retired in 1973, scored 31,419 points during his 14-year NBA career.) The game was stopped and the crowd gave the 7-foot-2 center a long ovation.

While Chamberlain used his sheer size and awesome strength to dominate the league, Abdul-Jabbar used grace and a soft touch to beat his opponents. Following a spectacular college career, during which he led the University of California–Los Angeles (UCLA) to an 88–2 record and three national championships, Abdul-Jabbar joined the Milwaukee Bucks of the NBA and led them to the league championship in 1971. He joined the Lakers in 1975, and helped them win championships in 1980, '82, '85, '87 and '88.

Pat Riley, Abdul-Jabbar's coach with the Lakers, called his center's skyhook "the greatest weapon of one person who's ever been an athlete in any sport."

Celtics Beat Lakers in NBA Finals . . . Again

For the first time in the Magic Johnson–Larry Bird era, the Los Angeles Lakers met the Boston Celtics in the NBA finals. The two teams had a longstanding rivalry that had one again been sparked, this time by the two dominant players in the league.

Playing in front of the home crowd in the Boston Garden for the seventh and deciding game of the series on June 12, the Celtics captured their 15th NBA title, beating the Lakers 111–102. The Celtics had never lost in the seventh game of a championship series.

Boston's forwards, Cedric Maxwell and Larry Bird, and their center, Robert Parish combined to pulled down 36 rebounds, more than the entire Lakers team. In fact, Boston outrebounded Los Angeles by a commanding 52–33 margin.

Leading throughout, the Celtics scored the last six points of the game to lock up the victory. Maxwell scored 24 points, while Bird poured in 20. Kareem Abdul-Jabbar was the high scorer for the Lakers, with 29 points.

Including the 1984 series, the two teams had met in the NBA finals eight times since the league began, and the Celtics won all eight times.

Stern Becomes NBA Commissioner

As the 1980s began, the popularity and reputation of the NBA was at a low. But the "Magic and Bird Show," reigniting the classic Celtics-Lakers rivalry, coupled with the arrival of Michael Jordan in 1985, jump-started interest in the league and began its revival.

Then David Stern took over as league commissioner. As it turned out, he was the perfect executive to maximize and capitalize on the league's growing popularity. First, he orchestrated a deal that created an NBA salary cap, setting a limit on how much each team could pay their players. This cap protected owners from endlessly skyrocketing payrolls, while guaranteeing players 53 percent of gross revenues. The agreement helped the NBA avoid the labor disputes that plagued baseball and football (and continue to plague baseball).

Under Stern's guidance, the league started marketing itself to a younger, more ethnically diverse fan base, tapping into hip-hop culture and consciously changing NBA basketball games into sports-and-entertainment events. The annual All-Star Game became All-Star Weekend, with popular slam-dunk and three-point contests, and the televised draft lottery increased fan interest in each year's crop of incoming college players.

With exciting, popular stars already in place, Stern was the final piece of the puzzle that brought the NBA to its greatest popularity in the 1980s and '90s.

Payton Passes Brown

There had never been a football running back like Jim Brown (b.1936). He combined speed, balance, agility, and explosive power, making him almost impossible to tackle. "All you do," said former New York Giants linebacker Sam Huff when asked how he approached tackling Brown, "is grab hold, hang on, and wait for help."

Sweetness

The Chicago Bears' Walter Payton combined amazing balance and power during his 13 years in the NFL (1975–1987) to rack up an astounding 16,726 rushing yards. That was a league record that stood until Dallas' Emmitt Smith surpassed it in 2002.

When a running back picks up 100 yards in a game, it's considered a great day. In a game against the Minnesota Vikings in 1977, Payton rushed for an NFL-record 275 yards. That mark stood for 23 years.

When faced with the choice between running out of bounds or colliding with a defensive player to try for a few extra yards, Payton put down his shoulder and bashed into his opponent, driving forward with an almost unstoppable force. He was as complete a player as has ever stepped onto a football field. In addition to his unmatched running ability, Payton also was a top-notch blocker and pass receiver. He could throw the ball well, too.

As intimidating as he was on the field, however, Payton earned his nickname "Sweetness" not only for his sweet moves, but also for his kind and playful temperament. Before Michael Jordan became Chicago's greatest sports hero, Payton was the most beloved athlete in town.

Sadly, in 1999, the Pro Football Hall of Famer (he was inducted in 1993, his first year of eligibility) was diagnosed with a rare liver disease. He died later that year, on November 1, shaking the entire sports world.

1984

During his nine seasons in the NFL (1957–1965) Brown led the league in rushing eight times, compiling a record 12,312 yards. After winning his second MVP award in 1965, Brown retired, preferring to go out at the top of his game.

On October 7, Brown's nearly 20-year-old career rushing record was shattered by the man they called "Sweetness." In the third quarter of a game against the New Orleans Saints, Chicago Bears running back Walter Payton took a pitchout (a play where the quarterback tosses the ball underhand to a back who is too far away to hand off to) from quarterback Jim McMahon and ran for six yards. Those yards pushed his 10-year career total past Brown's record.

When the game ended, Payton was mobbed by players from both teams, eager to offer congratulations to one of the most-loved professional athletes of all time (see the box on page 44). He finished that day with 154 yards, bringing his career total at the time to 12,400.

Payton broke another of Brown's records that day as well. He rushed for 100 yards or more for the 59th time of his career—one more than Brown had during his nine years in the NFL.

Colts Leave Town in the Dead of Night

The ever-tightening grip of business on sports was evident when, in a move that can only be described as sneaky, Baltimore Colts owner Robert Irsay moved his NFL franchise out of Baltimore and into Indianapolis on March 29, in the dead of night.

The secret operation stunned not only fans but also city officials, who, contrary to usual policy, had no idea the team planned to leave. Irsay, unhappy with his stadium lease and declining ticket sales in Baltimore, hired a fleet of vans to sneak over to the team's training facility and clean it out under cover of darkness. The vans then headed for Indianapolis, where Irsay decided to set up shop for the upcoming season. Indianapolis mayor William Hudnut announced the Colts' arrival, saying the team would play their future NFL games in the yet-to-be-completed, 60,000-seat Hoosier Dome.

It was known that Irsay had been negotiating with city officials in Indianapolis for several months before the move, but the suddenness of the departure caught everyone by surprise. With the entire team's possessions already moved to Indianapolis, there was nothing the state of Maryland could do.

Having lost a court case that allowed the Oakland Raiders to move to Los Angeles in 1982 (see page 33), the NFL decided to keep a low profile and chose to take no action. Fans in Baltimore were stunned and outraged, and would remain so until the arrival of a new NFL franchise, the Ravens, in 1996.

Soviet Union Boycotts Olympics

In an obvious payback for the U.S.-led boycott of the 1980 Olympics in Moscow, the Soviet Union and 13 of its allies boycotted the 1984 Summer Olympics in Los Angeles in August. Romania was the only Eastern European country in the

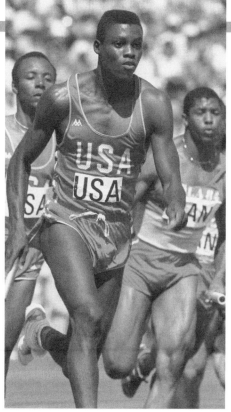

Good as Gold *Sixteen-year-old gymnast Mary Lou Retton (left) and sprinter Carl Lewis starred for the United States at the 1984 Olympic Games in Los Angeles.*

Soviet bloc to come to Los Angeles. The powerhouse team from East Germany, always among the tops in medals, was among those that stayed away.

A record 140 nations did show up, but without the usual competition from the Soviets and East Germans, the United States won a record 83 gold medals.

The Los Angeles Olympics were the first privately financed games ever, and they made a huge profit of $215 million. *Time* magazine was so impressed that it named organizing president Peter Ueberroth its Man of the Year.

U.S. Men Take Gymnastic Gold

The American men's gymnastic team gave an inspired performance at the Summer Games in Los Angeles, capturing the gold medal in the all-around team competition.

The six-man squad of Peter Vidmar, Bart Conner, Mitch Gaylord, Tim Daggett, James Hartung, and Scott Johnson edged the world-champion Chinese team, which many thought was unbeatable, by just 0.6 points.

1984

After five of the six events, the Americans held a small lead over the Chinese team. They were trying to win the first gold medal in gymnastics ever by a U.S. squad. Going with riskier but higher-scoring moves, the United States six held together, finishing the final event, the horizontal bars, with a perfect 10 for Daggett. The gold was finally theirs!

Meanwhile, on the women's team, a 4-foot-9, 94-pound, 16-year-old named Mary Lou Retton led the American women to a silver medal in the team competition. She charmed the fans and instantly became America's sweetheart. Retton then took America's second gymnastics gold medal,

becoming the first American woman to do so, by winning the individual all-around competition. She wrapped up her performance with back-to-back perfect scores of 10 on both her vaults.

Lewis Wins Four More Golds

U.S. track and field star Carl Lewis won gold medals at the Summer Olympics in the same four events that Jesse Owens had won 48 years earlier at the 1936 Olympics in Berlin. His golden grand slam established Lewis as the top athlete at the Games in Los Angeles.

Other Milestones of 1984

✔ On April 13, Pete Rose became only the second player in baseball history to reach 4,000 career hits. He trailed only all-time hits leader Ty Cobb (1886–1961), who had 4,191 hits in his Major League Baseball career.

✔ Victoria Roche became the first girl to play in the Little League World Series in Williamsport, Pennsylvania, in August.

✔ Kirk Gibson's World Series home run heroics helped the Detroit Tigers win the Series in five games. In game five on October 14, against the San Diego Padres, Gibson hit two homers and drove in five runs to lead the Tigers to an 8–4 Series-clinching victory.

Kirk Gibson

✔ Martina Navratilova continued her dominance of women's tennis, winning 78 of her 80 matches.

✔ Senda Berenson Abbott, Bertha Teague, and Margaret Wade became the first three women inducted into the Basketball Hall of Fame.

✔ The United States Supreme Court ruled that the NFL could not prevent its teams from moving from one city to another.

✔ The United States Supreme Court ruled that the NCAA's exclusive control over television coverage of college football violated the Sherman Antitrust Act, which outlaws monopolies.

In the 100-meter sprint, Lewis came from behind to take the event in 9.99 seconds, beating his teammate, Sam Graddy. Next up was the long jump, where he leaped 28 feet, 1/4 inch on his first try. He passed on the remaining four jumps to conserve energy, and his jump held up for another gold.

In the 200-meter sprint, Lewis led a United States sweep, winning the gold in 19.80 seconds—an Olympic record. American Kirk Baptiste took the silver with a time of 19.96 seconds, and Thomas Jefferson captured bronze with a time of 20.26 seconds to complete the U.S. sweep.

Lewis completed his grand slam as part of the 4-by-100-meter relay team, joining Graddy, Ron Brown, and Calvin Smith in setting a world record with a time of 37.83 seconds.

First Women's Olympic Marathon

The first women's marathon in Olympic history was held at the Los Angeles Games on August 5. American Joan Benoit Samuelson, a two-time Boston Marathon winner and world-record holder in the event, won the inaugural race in two hours, 24 minutes, 53 seconds. Samuelson's gold medal time was not only the third best time ever run by a woman in any marathon, but would actually have taken the gold medal in 13 of the previous 20 Olympic marathons run by men.

Amazingly, America's newest golden hero almost didn't make it to the Games. Two and half weeks before the Olympic trials in May, she injured her right knee and underwent arthroscopic surgery. Intense physical therapy and cardiovascular conditioning (she pedaled an exercise bike with her hands) enabled her to win the Olympic trials just 17 days after her knee surgery.

As the first women's marathon in Olympic history began, many spectators lining the route wept with joy, realizing that the long struggle to achieve recognition for women's long-distance running had finally borne fruit. Just 14 minutes into the race, Samuelson pulled away from the pack and never looked back.

Half a mile from the Los Angeles Coliseum, where the long race would finally end, she passed a large mural depicting her victory at the Boston Marathon. As she entered the tunnel leading to the Coliseum's track, where she would complete her final lap, Benoit Samuelson hoped her achievement would announce to the world that women belonged among the ranks of great long-distance runners.

As she appeared in the stadium and took her final lap around the track, 50,000 screaming fans rose and cheered the lone figure who finished the race 400 meters (and more than minute) ahead of the rest of the field. The world of long-distance running would never be the same.

1985

Jordan Endorsement Triggers "Sneaker Wars"

On the court, Chicago Bulls rookie Michael Jordan established himself as the NBA's hot new star. He averaged 28.2 points per game on his way to winning the Rookie of the Year award. Off the court, Jordan signed an endorsement deal for a new line of Nike shoes called Air Jordans. Sports marketing, endorsement dollars, and urban fashion would never be the same.

Naming an athletic shoe after a top professional athlete ushered in the age of big-time athlete endorsements. As a pro player—particularly a basketball player—rose in fame or entered the league as a touted rookie, marketing gurus and sneaker companies engaged in fierce competition to sign him up.

Every shoe company wanted to be associated with the next big star. Over the next decade, every company from Reebok to Adidas got into the act, scrambling to sign the big names. The so-called "Sneaker Wars" had begun. By the 1990s, big-time rookies were signing endorsement contracts that were even more lucrative than their sky-high NBA salaries.

Very quickly, owning Air Jordans, or whatever the latest athlete-endorsed shoe was, became a major status symbol among American youth. Even those who could not afford the high-priced shoes felt they had to have them. This led to incidents of boys and young men being robbed for their pricey sneakers.

For Jordan, the journey from simply being a great basketball player to becoming his own world-wide marketing brand had begun.

Montana Leads the 49ers to Another Super Bowl

Adding another chapter to his growing football legend, San Francisco 49ers quarterback Joe Montana led his team to its second Super Bowl victory in four years. Montana passed for three touchdowns and ran for another as the 49ers crushed the Miami Dolphins 38–16 in Super Bowl XIX at Stanford Stadium in Palo Alto, California on January 20.

Montana's first strike was a 33-yard touchdown pass to running back Carl Monroe in the first quarter. He hit running back Roger Craig, his favorite target of the day, in the second quarter for an eight-

Ready for Takeoff *The NBA career of Chicago Bulls rookie Michael Jordan (23) got off to a flying start—and the "Sneaker Wars" among shoe companies soon followed.*

yard touchdown, and again in the third quarter for a 16-yard scoring pass. The crafty quarterback also ran the ball in from the six-yard line for a touchdown in the second quarter.

Montana finished the day with 24 completions in 35 attempts for 331 yards—a Super Bowl record—and he was not intercepted. He also rushed for a game-best 59 yards.

Eight Is Enough *After losing to the Boston Celtics in all eight of their previous meetings in the NBA Finals, the Los Angeles Lakers, led by guard Earvin (Magic) Johnson, finally subdued their long-time rivals.*

Montana's backfield helped the cause, as Wendell Tyler rushed for 65 yards and Roger Craig ran for 58 yards to go with the 77 he gained catching seven of Montana's passes. Craig set a Super Bowl record by scoring three touchdowns.

Lakers Finally Beat Celtics in NBA Finals

Many professional athletes are superstitious. The members of the Los Angles Lakers must certainly have believed they had a jinx on them heading into the 1985 NBA finals against their longtime rival, the Boston Celtics.

This was the ninth time the two teams met in the finals, and Boston had won all eight of the previous series. In fact, the jinx extended back all the way to 1959, when the Lakers were playing in Minneapolis. But the Showtime Lakers of southern California finally broke the jinx, beating the Celtics in six games. Los Angeles took the deciding game 111–100 in front of a hostile crowd at Boston Garden on June 9.

The Celtics were trying to become the first team to win back-to-back NBA championships since they did it themselves in 1967–68 and 1968–69. But this year, Magic Johnson, Kareem Abdul-Jabbar, James Worthy, and the rest of the Lakers proved too much for Larry Bird, Kevin McHale, Robert Parish, and their teammates.

Heading into the sixth game in Boston, the Lakers held a 3–2 advantage in the Finals. The Celtics were hoping to tie the series and force a seventh and deciding game—something they had never

Meanwhile, the tough 49ers' defense swarmed all over Dolphins quarterback Dan Marino, forcing him to rush passes and throw two interceptions. Marino completed 29 of his 50 passes for a total of 318 yards and one touchdown, but Miami could muster little other offense.

lost. But Jabbar poured in 29 points and Worthy, who averaged 23.6 points and shot 56.4 percent from the field in the series, added 28. Johnson, who averaged 18.3 points, 14 assists, and 6.8 rebounds in the series, ran the offense.

The game was tied at halftime. The Lakers opened the second half by hitting their first six shots, putting them in control, despite 32 points from McHale and 28 from Bird. What made this victory even sweeter was the fact that the Celtics had crushed the Lakers 148–114 in the series opener, setting the stage for yet another Celtics' championship. But this year, it was not to be.

Thirty-eight-year-old Jabbar, the oldest player in the NBA, was just 12 in 1959, when the jinx began. In 1985 he was the big factor in finally shattering the Celtic's grip on the Lakers.

"You are never going to see another one like him," Lakers coach Pat Riley told *The Sporting News* after game six, speaking of Jabbar. "He is a superior athlete, the best of our time. Without him, we're just an ordinary team."

With him, the Lakers finally beat the Celtics in the NBA Finals.

1985 NBA Finals

GAME	LOCATION	SCORE
1	Boston	Celtics, 148–114
2	Boston	Lakers, 109–102
3	Los Angeles	Lakers, 136–111
4	Los Angeles	Celtics, 107–105
5	Los Angeles	Lakers, 120–111
6	Boston	Lakers, 111–100

Knight's Chair Toss

Indiana University basketball coach Bobby Knight was always known as much for his hot temper as for his success on the court. During a game against University of Illinois, which Indiana lost 66–50, Knight broke a chair in a fit of rage, then made an obscene gesture at the referee—a frequent target of Knight's outbursts.

Later, in a game against Purdue University on February 23, which Indiana also lost, Knight picked up a chair and hurled it across the court, then shouted at the referee as Purdue's Steve Reid was getting ready to shoot a technical foul shot. Knight was immediately ejected from the game.

A few days later, Knight apologized, saying his action was an embarrassment to the university. He explained that he was frustrated by the officiating and lost his temper. This pattern of major tantrums and verbal abuse was repeated throughout his tenure at Indiana.

Knight's most infamous explosion occurred when he was coaching the United States team in the Pan American Games in 1979. During that tournament, Knight hit a policeman in Puerto Rico, creating an international incident. That same year, Knight threw a student newspaper photographer into the bushes because the student took his picture while he was having an argument with a bicyclist about who had the right of way.

Finally, after 29 years at Indiana, during which time he led his teams to 763 victories and three national championships, Knight was fired in September of 2000 for

Magic Johnson: The First Triple Threat

Magic Johnson blurred the lines between the three positions in basketball: guard, forward, and center. He was the tallest point guard (the guard who brings the ball down the court and runs the offense) in the history of the NBA. He also excelled at forward and center. In game seven of the NBA Finals in 1980, Johnson's rookie year, he filled in at center for future Hall-of-Fame teammate Kareem Abdul-Jabbar and dominated the game, helping his team win the championship (see page 13).

Johnson quickly became the master of the triple-double—achieving double figures in points, rebounds, and assists in the same game—another demonstration of his versatility. But perhaps his biggest contribution was that he brought a team concept to the NBA at a time when most players were concentrating on their individual performances.

Johnson had enough talent to be a one-man show, but he preferred to make his teammates look good and to use his abilities to forge a winning team. His five NBA titles prove he did just that.

In 1991, Johnson's impact moved beyond the world of sports when he announced to a startled world that he had tested positive for HIV, the virus that causes AIDS. He put a familiar, trusted, beloved, celebrity face on the disease, helping to bring greater acceptance and understanding of the people who live with it.

allegedly grabbing a student by the arm because he addressed the coach as "Knight," and Knight felt that was disrespectful. In truth, it was the last straw in his long list of offenses.

Gretzky Breaks 200 Points—Again

Wayne Gretzky broke the previously unimaginable 200-point mark for the third time in his NHL career, scoring 73 goals and dishing out 135 assists, for a total of 208 points. He also won his unprecedented sixth consecutive MVP Award.

Most important, though, he led the Edmonton Oilers to their second straight Stanley Cup Championship, beating the Philadelphia Flyers in five games. In the deciding game on May 30, Gretzky scored a goal and had three assists in the Oilers'

8–3 victory. He got help from defenseman Paul Coffey, who added two goals.

Edmonton's Jari Kurri scored early in the first period. Thirty-five seconds later, Willie Lindstrom knocked in a shot to give the Oilers a two-goal cushion. Two more goals by Coffey in less than three minutes pushed the lead to 4–0. By the end of the second period, the Oilers were up 6–1.

Gretzky scored in the final period to finish the postseason with 47 points (17 goals, 30 assists), an NHL playoff record. The Oilers were on top again, thanks to the Great One.

Rose Is Baseball's All-Time Hits Leader

Pete Rose became baseball's all-time hits leader when he picked up his 4,192nd career hit, passing legendary

Hall-of-Famer Ty Cobb's career record. On September 11, the player known as "Charlie Hustle" broke the record he had been chasing since he first put on a Major League Baseball uniform in 1963.

Rose only played the game one way: hard. He pushed himself in the field, on the bases, and at bat. When the Cincinnati Reds needed a hit, there was Rose to slap the ball the other way, slashing it into the corner from either side of the plate, not bothering to slow down at first base, diving headlong into second.

With two balls and one strike on Rose, San Diego Padres pitcher Eric Show threw a fastball and Rose swung the familiar swing baseball fans had seen so many times before, and hit a clean single to left field. Baseball had a new hits leader. The chase was over. Rose had finally caught Cobb, who retired from baseball in 1928. In fact, Rose got his record-breaking hit 57 years to the day after Cobb's final major-league game.

Rose dashed from the batter's box, as he always did, rounding first swiftly, then scooting back to the bag. The game was stopped as flashbulbs went off all over Riverfront Stadium in Cincinnati.

Rose's 15-year-old son, Petey, reached his dad first, as players from both teams poured from the dugouts and gathered around the 44-year-old Cincinnati native. Tears streamed down his face, as he looked skyward and thought of two men who could not be there with him that day: his father, a semi-pro football player who was the biggest influence on Rose's life and his career in sports; and Cobb, whose achievement had haunted Rose through more than 20 major-league seasons.

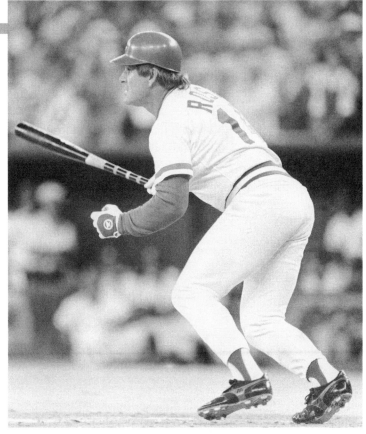

Historic Hit *Cincinnati Reds first baseman Pete Rose watches the 4,192nd hit of his career fall safely into the outfield. With the single, Rose broke Ty Cobb's big-league record for career hits.*

Royals Win By Decision

The Kansas City Royals outlasted the St. Louis Cardinals in seven games to win a wild World Series that turned on an umpire's pivotal call at first base in game six.

Kansas City had reached the Series in dramatic fashion. First, the Royals edged the California Angels to win the American League West by a single game. Then, they rallied from a three games to one deficit by winning three consecutive games and beating the Toronto Blue Jays in seven

1985

games in the American League Championship Series (ALCS).

In the National League, the Cardinals won a major-league-best 101 games during the regular season, then qualified for the Fall Classic when Jack Clark belted a three-run home run in the ninth inning to win the sixth, and final, game of the National League Championship Series (NLCS) against the Los Angeles Dodgers.

The drama carried over to the World Series. St. Louis won a taut opening game,

then scored four times in the ninth inning of game two to rally for a 4–2 victory and take a commanding lead in the Series. The Cardinals still held a three-games-to-two lead and were three outs away from a championship when they carried a 1–0 lead into the bottom of the ninth inning of game six at Kansas City.

Pinch-hitter Jorge Orta led off the ninth inning for the Royals and quickly fell behind no balls and two strikes. Then he grounded to Clark at first base, who threw to pitcher Todd Worrell covering for an apparent out. But umpire Don Denkinger ruled Orta safe—though television replays clearly indicated it was the wrong call. The Cardinals then came unglued. Clark misplayed a foul pop that should have been caught, and a single, a passed ball, and Dane Iorg's single won the game for the Royals, 2–1.

Game seven the next night was no contest. The Royals scored twice in the second inning and three more times in the third to open a 5–0 advantage. In the fifth, the Cardinals lost their composure. Pitcher Joaquin Andujar was ejected during a six-run outburst by the Royals, who went on to win 11–0.

Women's Pioneer

The Women's Sports Foundation named Libby Riddles its Professional Sportswoman of the Year for 1985. Riddles had made history earlier in the year, on March 20, when she became the first woman ever to win the Iditarod Sled Dog Race in Alaska.

The Iditarod is a grueling test of endurance in which competitors guide a

Frontier Woman *Libby Riddles became the first woman to win the grueling Iditarod Sled Dog Race.*

Other Milestones of 1985

✔ The 45-second shot clock was added to college basketball to help speed up the game.

✔ On July 11, Nolan Ryan became the first pitcher in baseball history to strike out 4,000 batters.

✔ Future Hall-of-Fame pitcher Tom Seaver won his 300th game on August 4 for the Chicago White Sox, becoming only the 17th player in Major League Baseball history to do so.

✔ On August 21, Mary Decker set a new women's record, running the mile in 4 minutes, 16.71 seconds. She broke the old mark of 4 minutes, 17.44 seconds by Maricica Puica of Romania.

Eddie Robinson

✔ Grambling State University football coach Eddie Robinson passed Paul "Bear" Bryant, with his 324th victory on November 23, to become the winningest coach in the history of college football.

✔ The North American Soccer League, the latest unsuccessful attempt at a pro soccer league in the United States, suspended operations after 18 years.

✔ The NFL's Chicago Bears rode a dominating defense to win 15 of 16 games during the regular season and reach the Super Bowl.

team of dogs more than 1,050 miles through beautiful, but rugged, terrain that includes mountain ranges, rivers, and forest, often in the harshest weather. Riddles, in fact, had to navigate through a deadly blizzard across Norton Sound en route to her victory.

Susan Butcher followed Riddles' historic victory by winning the Iditarod each of the next three years.

1986

Baseball Suspends Seven Players for Drug Use

Drug use continued to invade the world of sports—this time Major League Baseball. Baseball commissioner Peter Ueberroth handed out one-year suspensions to seven players, saying that they had used drugs themselves or aided in spreading drugs within baseball.

Keith Hernandez (New York Mets), Dale Berra (New York Yankees), Joaquin Andujar (Oakland Athletics), Dave Parker (Cincinnati Reds), Jeffrey Leonard (San Francisco Giants), Lonnie Smith (Kansas City Royals), and Enos Cabell (Los Angeles Dodgers) were all suspended without pay.

All seven players chose an alternative penalty offered by Ueberroth, which resulted in the lifting of the suspensions. The players agreed to give 10 percent of their salaries for the 1986 season to drug-prevention programs, and to put in up to 200 hours of community service over the next two years. They also agreed to undergo drug tests for the remainder of their major-league careers.

The players either testified or were implicated during the 1985 investigations and trials of seven men charged with distributing cocaine. Although none of the players was charged in those trials, six of the seven gave incriminating testimony. The seventh, Andujar, was named by several players as a cocaine user.

In an attempt to stem the spreading tide of drug use, Ueberroth also gave out lesser penalties to 14 other players.

Bird Leads Celtics Back to NBA Title

Last year it was Magic Johnson's turn. He helped the Los Angeles Lakers break a 26-year jinx in the NBA Finals (see page 52), leading them to the championship over the Boston Celtics. This year it was Larry Bird's turn.

The Boston forward ranked among the league leaders in scoring (25.8 points per game), rebounding (9.8 rebounds per game), steals (2.02 steals per game), free-throw percentage (89.6 percent), and three-point-field-goal percentage (42.3 percent). He won his third straight NBA Most Valuable Player award, joining former Celtics' great Bill Russell and former Celtics' archrival Wilt Chamberlain as the only players in NBA history to win the

Baseball's Drug Scandal *The New York Mets' Keith Hernandez (right) faces the media.*

award three years in a row. And he helped Boston take back the NBA championship.

One of the main reason's for Bird's and the Celtics' success was a trade that brought veteran center Bill Walton to Boston. This gave the Celtics' already strong front court of Bird, Kevin McHale, and Robert Parish another top scorer, passer, rebounder, and defender. The addition of Walton also gave Parish some much-needed rest at center. Walton was an unselfish and team-oriented player — much like Bird. When the two were on the court together, the ball seemed to fly everywhere, always eventually finding an open man.

In the regular season the team won 67 games, the most ever for the famous Celtics. At home, they were virtually unbeatable, posting a regular-season record

Sweet Sixteen *Forward Larry Bird, the NBA's most valuable player for the third consecutive season, led the Boston Celtics to the league championship. It was the Celtics' record 16th title.*

final round of the Western Conference playoffs to gain a berth in the NBA Finals.

Boston dominated the June finals, beating Houston in six games. The Celtics took the last game by a score of 114–97. Bird recorded in a triple-double (29 points, 11 rebounds, 12 assists) and was voted the NBA Finals' MVP. The championship was Boston's second in three years, the team's 16th overall, and the last title of the Bird era.

The following year, it would be Magic's turn again.

College Star Dies From Cocaine

Twenty-two year old Len Bias, an All-American basketball star at the University of Maryland, died on June 19 from using cocaine—just two days after being selected by the Boston Celtics as the number-two pick in the NBA draft.

The 6-foot-8 Bias was Maryland's all-time leading scorer, with 2,149 points during his college career. He averaged 23.3 points per game, pulled down 224 rebounds, and was voted the Atlantic Coast Conference's Player of the Year during his final season.

After an exciting day in Boston, during which Bias was introduced as the Celtics' next great star, Bias returned to the Maryland campus. The following night, he was with two teammates when he died suddenly. Autopsy reports showed that he died of intoxication from cocaine, which he most likely snorted only minutes before his death. The sports world was shocked at the tragic loss of a young life and a potential NBA great.

of 40–1 at the Boston Garden. Then they went 10–0 at home in the playoffs.

Boston blew through the early rounds of the playoffs, losing only one game, as they cruised toward a much-anticipated rematch with the Lakers. But the powerful Houston Rockets, led by a pair of seven-footers—Ralph Sampson and Hakeem Olajuwon, together known as the "Twin Towers"—beat the Lakers in the

USFL Loses Lawsuit, Closes Shop

After three years as a professional football league, trying to compete with the NFL for players and fans, the United States Football League (USFL) disbanded, calling off its 1986 season.

The league began in 1983 with 12 teams, and for three years had played a spring schedule to avoid going head-to-head with the NFL's fall games. But in 1986, the USFL decided to switch to a fall schedule and compete directly with the older league.

After trying unsuccessfully to get a television contract—a must for the survival of any professional sports league—the USFL filed a lawsuit against the NFL, claiming that it monopolized the television networks and prevented the younger league from getting a contract to broadcast their games. The USFL asked for more than $1 billion in damages.

Following a long trial, a jury ruled that although the NFL was a professional monopoly, it had done nothing to keep the USFL off the air. That decision had been made by the networks themselves. Damages were awarded to the USFL in the amount of $1.

Without big money from the lawsuit or a television contract, USFL team owners felt they could not continue operating. The league had already lost more than $150 million in its first three seasons. Six days after the suit ended, the league's remaining eight teams voted to cease operations.

Running back Herschel Walker, the USFL's biggest star and greatest hope for success, signed a five-year contact with the NFL's Dallas Cowboys.

Joyner Sets Heptathlon Record

Jackie Joyner (b.1962), who won the silver medal in the heptathlon at the 1984 Olympics and went on to take the gold in the event in 1988, set a new world record in the heptathlon at the Goodwill Games in Moscow on July 7, smashing individual event records along the way.

Bird Flies

At a time in the NBA when high-flying schoolyard moves and flashy slam dunks were the norm, forward Larry Bird stepped onto the parquet floor at the Boston Garden and did something that had not been seen in the league in awhile. He made his teammates better.

After a stunning college career at Indiana State University, capped by a college player of the year award in his senior year and a memorable showdown in the NCAA championship game against Magic Johnson's Michigan State team (won by Johnson and Michigan State), Bird joined the Boston Celtics.

The once-great NBA dynasty was struggling through a low period. In his rookie season, Bird led his team to 32 more victories than the previous year. He went on to win three NBA championships, three consecutive Most Valuable Player awards, and, along with Magic Johnson, reinvigorate interest in the NBA.

After playing with the United States Olympic "Dream Team" in Barcelona, Spain in 1992, Bird retired as a player, due to a bad back. He went on to become a successful professional coach with the Indiana Pacers. In 1998, he was enshrined in basketball's Hall of Fame.

1986

Joyner totaled 7,148 points, becoming the first woman to break the 7,000-point mark in the grueling seven-event competition, and beating the record set by Sabine Paetz of East Germany in 1984 by 202 points.

The heptathlon is a two-day competition made up of seven events: the 100-meter hurdles, the shot put, the high jump, the 200-meter race, the long jump, the javelin, and the 800-meter race.

Joyner set a first-day record by scoring 4,151 points in four events. She ran the 100-meter hurdles in 12.85 seconds, a new American heptathlon record. Then she leaped 62 inches in the high jump; threw the shot put 48 feet, 5 1/4 inches; and ran the 200 meters in 23 seconds.

The second day of competition began with Joyner setting a heptathlon world record by jumping 23 feet in the long jump, her favorite event. She then tossed the javelin 163 feet, 4 inches.

In the final event, Joyner ran the 800-meter race in 2 minutes, 10.02 seconds to capture the heptathlon record. Despite the United States' boycott of the Olympics in Moscow in 1980 and the Soviet boycott of the Games in Los Angeles in 1984, the American was cheered wildly by Goodwill Games fans in Moscow as she set the new standard in her sport.

One Strike Away

The 1986 Major League Baseball playoffs—the American League Championship Series (ALCS), the National League Championship Series (NLCS), and the World Series—were among the most exciting and memorable in baseball history.

Boston Red Sox fans cheered their team to a great regular season, but October 12 they appeared to once again be watching their beloved Sox get eliminated in the post season. The California Angels led the ALCS three games to one, and led game five by a score of 5–2 entering the top of the ninth inning. The Red Sox scored two runs, but still trailed by a run with two outs in the ninth.

Boston centerfielder Dave Henderson came up to bat with a man on base, facing the Angels' top relief pitcher, Donnie Moore. Henderson worked the count to two balls and two strikes, bringing the Red Sox's season one strike away from ending. He fouled off two pitches to keep the game going, the drama building, and the Boston season alive.

Hendersen drove Moore's next pitch into the stands in left field for a two-run homer that gave Boston the lead, 6–5. Although the Angels came back to tie the game in the bottom of the ninth inning, the Red Sox scored again in the 11th inning to win 7–6, cutting California's lead in the series to three games to two.

The Angels never recovered from losing the game after being one strike away from victory and a trip to the World Series. Boston won the next two games easily by scores of 10–4 and 8–1, to take the ALCS and earn a spot in the October Series.

Meanwhile, in the NLCS, the New York Mets battled the Houston Astros, who were led by pitcher Mike Scott. Scott won 18 games during the regular season while leading the league with 306 strikeouts and a 2.22 earned run average (ERA—the average number of runs charged to the pitcher per nine innings).

He was named the National League Cy Young Award winner and the NLCS Most Valuable Player in 1985, despite the fact that his team lost the playoff series.

Scott dominated the Mets, shutting them out 1–0 in game one, then taking a 3–1 victory in game four. Heading into game six in Houston on October 15, the Mets led the series three games to two. If they lost game six, they would have to face Scott again in a deciding game seven—a fate they were hoping to avoid.

The Astros jumped out to a 3–0 lead in the first inning, then Houston pitcher Bob Knepper shut down the Mets for eight innings. New York finally scored three times in the top of the ninth to tie the game and send it into extra innings.

The Mets scored a run in the top of the 14th inning, but Houston tied it in the bottom of the 14th. Then, in the top of the 16th inning, New York scored three runs to grab what seemed to be a commanding 7–4 lead. Houston came back to score two in the bottom of the 16th, and had the tying run on second base when Mets relief pitcher Jesse Orosco struck out Houston rightfielder Kevin Bass to end the marathon and send the Mets to the World Series.

But the exciting ALCS and NLCS were only prelude to the astounding World Series still to come.

The Red Sox won the first two games in New York, then the Mets returned the favor, taking the next two in Boston. The Red Sox jumped out to a three-games-to-two lead, winning game five 4–2 in Boston.

The series returned to New York for game six on October 25, with the Red Sox one win away from capturing their first World Series since 1918. The game was tied 3–3 after nine innings, but Boston took the lead in the top of the 10th, scoring two runs.

The first two Mets to bat in the bottom of the 10th inning were easily retired by Boston relief pitcher Calvin Schiraldi. Then Gary Carter and Kevin Mitchell both hit singles. The next batter, Ray Knight, fell behind in the count 0–2. Just as they were one strike away from elimination in the ALCS, the Red Sox were now one strike away from winning the World Series.

Knight singled to center, scoring Carter and cutting the Boston lead to 5–4. Mitchell moved to third base. The Red Sox brought in a new pitcher, Bob Stanley, to face Mookie Wilson, in what turned out to be one of the most famous at-bats in World Series history.

Wilson worked the count to 2–2, and once again Boston was one strike away from victory. But Wilson kept fouling off

No Rush Hour in New York

Game six of the NLCS began at 3:06 p.m. New York time, and finally ended at 7:48. There was no rush hour in usually busy New York City that night, as office workers stayed in their offices to catch the end of this seemingly endless game.

Buses and subways were half empty, though announcements at Grand Central Station kept the few commuters who did head home updated on the score. People on the street gathered around anyone who had a radio, or huddled outside the windows of appliance stores that had TV sets on, unable to leave for fear of missing the latest twist or turn.

The great city slowed down to linger and learn the fate of its beloved Mets.

1986

pitches. Stanley's seventh pitch was wild, scoring Mitchell from third and tying the game at 5–5.

Three pitches later, Wilson hit a ground ball that dribbled through the legs of Boston first baseman Bill Buckner, scoring Knight with the winning run, setting off a wild celebration among the Mets' players, and tying the Series at three games apiece.

The 36-year-old Buckner normally would have been removed from the game in favor of a defensive replacement. But he had played such an important role in the Red Sox's success (he drove in 102 runs during the regular season) that Boston manager John McNamara left him in the game so he could enjoy the presumed victory celebration.

Stunned, like the Angels were after Boston's dramatic ALCS victory, the Red Sox lost game seven by a score of 8–5 and the Mets won the World Series, capping off an unforgettable post-season.

Sports Marketing Grows Into a Giant

S As a direct result of the increasing connection between professional sports and athlete-endorsed products, sneaker manufacturer Nike topped the billion-dollar mark in revenue for the first time in its history.

Nike, makers of the famous Air Jordan basketball shoe, extended its product line and its enormous sports marketing reach beyond sneakers and into the apparel business. The company introduced clothing collections endorsed by NBA star Michael Jordan and tennis great John McEnroe.

Nike's revenue and the impact of the world of celebrity endorsements continued to grow in the coming decades.

LeMond Is First American to Win the Tour de France

It is considered by many to be the largest, most important, and most difficult sporting event in the world. The Tour de France is a grueling 21-day bicycle race in which cyclists ride between 100 and 150 miles each day, often up steep and winding mountain roads.

An American in Paris *Greg LeMond became the first man from the United States to win the Tour de France, cycling's most important event and one of the most famous athletic competitions in the world.*

Other Milestones of 1986

✔ Following their overwhelming 46–10 victory against the New England Patriots in Super Bowl XX on January 26, the Chicago Bears made the first sports music video, "The Super Bowl Shuffle."

✔ On February 8, Debi Thomas became the first African-American figure skater to win the world championship.

✔ Jack Nicklaus won his sixth Augusta National Masters Golf Tournament in April, at the "ripe old" age of 46.

✔ Bill James published his *Historical Baseball Abstract*, a groundbreaking book with insightful statistical analysis.

✔ Boston Red Sox pitcher Roger Clemens struck out 20 Seattle Mariners' batters during his team's 3–1 victory at Fenway Park on April 29, setting a new single-game record (a decade later, in 1996, Clemens tied his own mark by striking out 20 Detroit Tigers in a game). The old mark of 19 was held by four players. Clemens also won both the Cy Young and AL MVP awards in 1986.

✔ Nancy Lieberman became the first woman to play in a men's basketball league when she joined the United States Basketball League's Springfield Fame.

✔ The three-point field goal was introduced in college basketball.

✔ The NFL approved the use of instant replay as a tool to aid officials, who could reverse their decisions on certain calls after reviewing visual evidence.

✔ Wayne Gretzky scored his 500th goal on November 22 while breaking his single-season scoring record of 212 points; he racked up 214 points.

Mike Tyson

✔ Also on November 22, 20-year-old boxer Mike Tyson knocked out Trevor Berbick to become the youngest heavyweight boxing champion in history.

On July 27, Greg LeMond became the first American to win this contest of strength, endurance, skill, and willpower. Battling teammate Bernard Hinault, as millions watched on television back in the United States, LeMond pedaled triumphantly into Paris and became an immediate media celebrity and American sports hero. LeMond was born June 26, 1961, in Los Angeles, making him 25 at the time of his Tour de France win.

A tragic hunting accident the following year almost cost LeMond his life, but set the stage for one of the most dramatic comebacks and human endurance stories ever, when he returned to win the Tour de France again in 1989.

1987

Simms Leads Giants to First Super Bowl Victory

Quarterback Phil Simms led the New York Giants to victory in Super Bowl XXI on January 25 in Pasadena, California with a second-half explosion that beat the Denver Broncos 39–20.

Tough defense dominated the first two quarters, and Denver took a 10–9 lead into the locker room at halftime. But Simms came out throwing at the start of the second half, tossing a 13-yard touchdown pass to Mark Bavaro. He then led the Giants down the field for a short field goal, followed by another drive capped by Joe Morris' one-yard touchdown run. Simms also threw a six-yard touchdown pass to Phil McConkey in the fourth quarter, putting the game out of reach at 33–10.

Simms was nearly flawless en route to earning the game's most valuable player award. He completed 22 of 25 passes (a record completion rate of 88 percent) for 268 yards and three touchdowns. Morris led the game's rushers with 67 yards. Denver quarterback John Elway passed for 304 yards, completing 22 of 37 attempts, but compiled most of the yardage during the first half.

Sugar Ray Comes Out of Retirement

In 1982, welterweight boxing champion Sugar Ray Leonard retired due to a detached retina in his left eye. Doctors told him that if he kept boxing, there was a chance he could lose vision in the eye.

On April 6, Leonard came out of retirement to battle World Boxing Council (WBC) middleweight champion Marvelous Marvin Hagler. The time away did not seem to diminish Leonard's great boxing skills. He danced, spun, and jabbed his way through the first few rounds, then stood toe-to-toe with Hagler, outslugging the champ as the fight drew to a close.

When it was over, the scores were close, but Leonard took a 12-round, split decision to capture the middleweight title. The more than 15,000 fans in the Las Vegas arena chanted his name, as Leonard earned his 34th victory in 35 fights. Hagler's record was 63–3, with 52 knockouts.

Dodger VP Resigns Over Racial Remarks

Seventy-year-old Al Campanis, vice president in charge of player per-

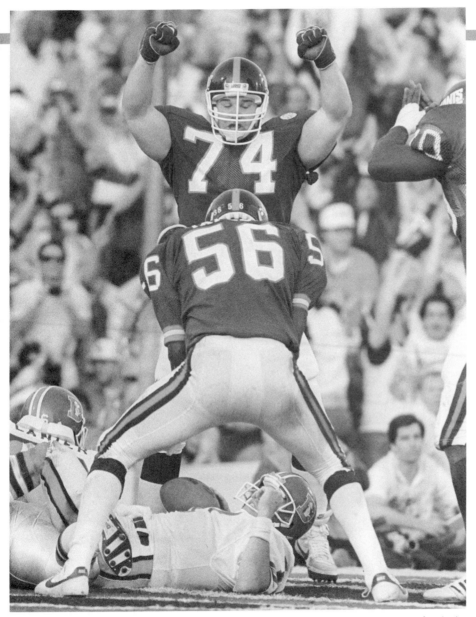

Safety in Numbers *Several New York Giants, including linebacker Lawrence Taylor (56), celebrate a safety in Super Bowl XXI against the Denver Broncos. The Giants won, 39–20.*

sonnel for baseball's Los Angeles Dodgers, resigned on April 8, following national outrage over remarks he made on the ABC television show *Nightline* two days earlier.

Campanis appeared on the show, hosted by Ted Koppel, to help celebrate the 40th anniversary of Jackie Robinson breaking baseball's color barrier. Koppel asked Campanis why he thought the

1987

major leagues had no black managers, general managers, or owners. Campanis replied, "I truly believe that they may not have some of the necessities to be, let's say, a field manager, or perhaps a GM."

When Koppel asked him if he really believed that, the Dodgers' vice president said, "Well, I don't say all of them, but they are short. How many quarterbacks do you have, how many pitchers do you have, that are black?" Then Campanis added, "Why are black men or black people not good swimmers? Because they don't have any buoyancy."

These comments set off a storm of controversy, forcing Campanis to apologize. He claimed that his statements were taken the wrong way and that he did not think blacks are less intelligent than whites. Two days after the remarks, however, Campanis resigned from the Dodgers.

He had been with the Dodgers' organization for 46 years, including seven games as a player in 1943. After serving in World War II, Campanis worked as a manager in the Dodgers' minor-league system. He became a scout in 1950 and director of scouting from 1957 to 1968, before finally settling in as a club vice president in 1969.

He had actually played as a minor leaguer with Robinson 41 years earlier, and helped to sign minority players such as Roberto Clemente and Tommy Davis, but his questionable comments on Nightline spelled the end of his lengthy baseball career.

Edwin Moses:
Perfect for the Sport

From the moment that Edwin Moses won the gold medal in the 400-meter intermediate (400 IM) hurdles at the 1976 Olympic Games, it was obvious to experts that he had the perfect physique for the event. His combination of size, speed, balance, and an amazing stride, both between the hurdles and going over them, was unique in the history of the sport.

Before Moses, most athletes who competed in the 400 IM took 14 strides between each hurdle over the first 200 meters of the race, then increased the number of strides to between 15 and 17 for the final 200 meters, as their muscles tired. Moses took 13 strides between hurdles over the entire 400-meter distance. And each of those strides was an amazing 9-foot-9.

Some people criticized Moses for not using a coach for most of his career, but Dr. Leroy Walker, his coach on the 1976 U.S. Olympic team, understood why. "Edwin's knowledge of the event is so infinite," Walker said at one point during the streak, "as to make any coach superfluous. All Ed needs is somebody to hold the watch."

Moses' Amazing Streak Finally Comes to an End

The most incredible winning streak in the history of track events finally came to an end 10 years after it had begun. Between 1977 and 1987, Edwin Moses won 122 consecutive races in the 400-meter intermediate hurdles (400 IM), setting what may be an unbeatable record.

In 1976, Moses won a gold medal in the event at the Munich, West Germany Olympics. The follow year, after a loss to West German Harald Schmid, his amazing winning streak began. As the streak grew longer, Moses took a track event that had lacked glamour and didn't get much attention, and brought it into the spotlight. Along the way, he became one of the sport's biggest stars.

For 10 years, there was no one even in the same class as Moses. He set the world record in the 400 IM at 47.02 seconds, and he also owns the next 10 fastest times in the event. The mental attitude Moses brought to each of the 122 races was as big a factor in his success as his extraordinary physical ability. "The day I feel nice and relaxed," Moses said in 1984, "is the day I'll know the streak is in danger."

Three years later, on June 4, a 21-year-old American hurdler named Danny Harris finally defeated the 31-year-old Moses in a 400 IM race. Harris took the lead at the fifth hurdle and finished with a time of 47.56 seconds. Moses finished right behind him, with a time of 47.69 seconds.

Moses smiled to the crowd of 11,000 in Madrid, Spain, who stood and chanted his name as the great champion ran a solo lap of honor around the track to celebrate his astounding streak.

Unser Wins His Fourth Indy 500

Al Unser, Sr., became the second driver in history to win the Indianapolis 500 four times when he captured the world's most prestigious motor race on May 24, winning by a margin of just five seconds. At age 47, Unser also became the oldest driver to win the race.

His previous victories came in 1970, 1971, and 1978. His four wins at Indy tied the record set by A.J. Foyt. Unser's 25-

All Four Won *Al Unser, Sr. won the Indianapolis 500 at the "Brickyard," the Indianapolis Motor Speedway. Unser joined A.J. Foyt as the only four-time winners of the world-renowned race.*

year-old son, Al Unser, Jr., finished fourth in the race.

The senior Unser averaged 162.175 miles per hour in front of the crowd of 400,000 racing fans at the Indianapolis Motor Speedway. The veteran drove in third place for most of the race, with Mario

1987

Andretti in the lead for 170 of the 200 laps, and Roberto Guerrero in second place, where he finished the race just seconds behind Unser.

During lap number 180, Andretti's engine failed, pulling him out of the race. Guerrero then made a rookie mistake during a pit stop that cost him an extra 55 seconds—enough to allow Unser to take the lead and eventually the race.

Gretzky Leads Oilers to Stanley Cup—Again

Wayne Gretzky won his unprecedented eighth consecutive Hart Memorial Trophy, the award given annually to the NHL's most valuable player. By decade's end he had won the award nine of 10 years. Gretzky also led his Edmonton Oilers to the Stanley Cup, the

Bo Knows Baseball . . . and Bo Knows Football *Bo Jackson already was a star for baseball's Kansas City Royals when he also signed to play football for the NFL's Los Angeles Raiders. He excelled at both sports.*

team's third NHL championship in four years.

In a well-played, seven-game final series, the Great One had some help in game seven to lock up the cup. Teammates Jari Kurri and Glen Anderson put the Oilers in the lead to stay with second- and third-period goals, respectively, as Edmonton beat the Philadelphia Flyers 3–1 on May 31 to capture the series. The Oilers' superb defensive play helped seal the victory.

Philadelphia goalie Ron Hextall had kept the underdog Flyers alive in the series with outstanding performances after the Oilers jumped out to a three-games-to-one lead. Led by Hextall's excellent goaltending, the Flyers bounced back to win game five 4–3 and game six 3–2 to tie the series, setting up the decisive seventh game.

In game seven, Hextall didn't get much help from his teammates, as he dealt with 43 Oilers' shots on goal, compared to only 20 shots faced by Edmonton goalie Grant Fuhr.

Bo Jackson Plays Two Pro Sports

🏆 Calling it a "hobby" to get him through the winter, pro baseball player Bo Jackson signed a five-year contract to play pro football with the Los Angeles Raiders. Jackson was already playing Major League Baseball for the Kansas City Royals. The agreement called for Jackson to join the Raiders at the end of the baseball season, which would allow him to play in about half of the team's 16 NFL games.

Two-Sport Superstar

By the time Bo Jackson—the 1985 Heisman Trophy winner as college football's top player—signed his first pro football contract, he had already established himself as an amazingly talented Major League Baseball player. He hit massive home runs nearing 500 feet in distance, made impossible throws from the deepest parts of ballparks, and climbed outfield walls to haul in long fly balls and take back home runs.

During the years that he played both professional sports, from 1987 through 1990, Jackson emerged as one of the most feared hitters in baseball and one of the fastest and most unstoppable running backs in the NFL.

A serious hip injury in 1991 ended his football career and cut short his baseball career. Others have played two sports, but no one has shown such ability in both.

In 1986, Jackson was the number-one overall pick in the NFL draft, but turned down a lucrative offer from the Tampa Bay Buccaneers. Instead, Jackson signed a deal with baseball's Royals and played with one of their minor-league teams.

His first full season in Major League Baseball was 1987. At the time he signed with the football Raiders—during baseball's All-Star break in July—Jackson was batting .254, with 18 homers and 45 runs batted in.

NFL Players Strike. . . Again

🏈 The National Football League Players Association went on strike two games into the 1987 season. The NFL players last staged a strike in 1982, when they shut down the game for 57 days (see page 31). This time, the players were hoping to gain unrestricted free agency—the

71

1987

right to sign with any team when a contract was up. They were also looking for a higher salary scale and increased pension benefits, as well as some minor contractual points.

The NFL responded by hiring replacement players. Games scheduled for the third weekend of the season were canceled, but the games in weeks four, five, and six were played with the replacement players.

The 24-day strike ended on October 15, and striking players returned for the seventh week of the season without a new contract, a back-to-work agreement, or a new collective bargaining agreement in place. Although some agreements were reached on minor issues, the major ques-

Other Milestones of 1987

✔ Three years after losing the America's Cup to Australia, an American skipper, Dennis Conner, regained it on February 4, sailing the ship *Stars & Stripes*.

✔ Woody Hayes, longtime football coaching great at Ohio State University, died on March 12 at age 74.

✔ In March, Susan Butcher won the Iditarod dogsled race in Alaska for the second year in a row. She was only one of two women in a field of 63 racers. Her time of 11 days, 2 hours, 5 minutes, and 13 seconds beat the race record by 13 hours.

✔ Philadelphia Phillies third baseman Mike Schmidt hit his 500th career home run on April 18, joining baseball's most elite group of sluggers.

✔ The Atlanta Braves started baseball's trend away from the pullover polyester uniforms of the 1970s and early '80s, going back to traditional button-up jerseys and returning to the team logo they had used 25 years earlier in Milwaukee.

Dennis Conner

✔ Julius Erving joined Wilt Chamberlain and Kareem Abdul-Jabbar as the only players in NBA history to score more than 30,000 career points.

✔ The Little League World Series celebrated its 40th anniversary in August.

✔ Magic Johnson was the NBA playoff MVP, leading the Los Angeles Lakers to their fourth title in eight years over the Boston Celtics.

✔ Two years after his Cy Young Award performance, New York Mets pitcher Dwight Gooden tested positive for drugs and entered a rehabilitation program.

✔ Mark McGwire of the Oakland Athletics set a record for baseball rookies with 49 home runs in his first season.

✔ On the title track of Public Enemy's debut album, "Yo! Bum Rush the Show," Chuck D rapped about the Chicago Bears' victory over the New England Patriots in Super Bowl XX.

tions of free agency, drug testing, and pension funding were left unresolved.

Rice Sets Two Records with One Catch

San Francisco 49ers wide receiver Jerry Rice set two NFL records with a single pass reception, catching a 20-yard touchdown pass from quarterback Steve Young in the third quarter of a game against the Atlanta Falcons on December 20.

The reception, Rice's 19th of the year, broke the record for the most touchdown catches in a season. It also marked the 12th consecutive game in which Rice had caught a touchdown pass, another NFL record.

By season's end, Rice had 22 touchdown receptions—a remarkable figure, especially given that he reached it in only 12 games because of the players' strike early in the year. But Rice, who was in his third NFL season after being selected in the first round of the 1985 draft, was just getting started. He would go on to become the most prolific touchdown scorer the league has ever known.

Rice played for the 49ers through the 2000 season, then joined the Oakland Raiders in 2001. Through 2003, his nineteenth year in the NFL (during which he turned 41 years old), he had scored 205 career touchdowns, far and away a league record. Running back Emmitt Smith was next on the list with 166.

1988

Golden Winter Olympics

At the 1988 Winter Olympics in Calgary, Canada in February—the first Olympic Games of the decade without a boycott of some kind—the United States came away with two gold medals. Both of these medals were hard fought, and both required near-perfect performances.

In men's figure skating, American Brian Boitano captured the gold medal in one of the closest competitions in Olympic history. Boitano beat Canadian Brian Orser by a slim margin, as the Canadian took the silver. Viktor Petrenko of the Soviet Union won the bronze. Boitano had a very narrow lead after the short program, leaving plenty of room for Orser to overtake him. But the American skated with great skill, showmanship, and emotion, delivering a stunning performance in the long program to secure his gold medal.

America's other gold came in women's speed skating. Bonnie Blair set a world record in the 500-meter sprint, capturing the gold with a time of 39.10 seconds. Blair knew she would have to skate a world's best time to win, having watched defending Olympic champion Christa Rothenburger of East Germany break her own world record just moments earlier in the competition. Rothenburger set the new record at 39.12 seconds. With that in mind, Blair skated to the gold, shaving Rothenburger's time by just two one-hundredths of a second.

Lakers Repeat NBA Title

After his team's victory in the 1987 NBA Finals over the Boston Celtics, Los Angeles Lakers head coach Pat Riley was asked if his team could win again the following year. No team had won back-to-back NBA championships since the Celtics did it in 1968 and 1969. "I'll guarantee it," Riley replied.

His team proved to be as good as his word. The Lakers needed seven games to beat the Detroit Pistons, but they captured their second straight NBA championship with a 108–105 victory in game seven, in front of their hometown fans, on June 21. The championship was the Lakers' fifth of the 1980s.

The Lakers had home-court advantage throughout the playoffs, thanks to a league-best 62–20 regular-season record, and they certainly needed it. Each of their other series—hard fought contests against

Close Call *Brian Boitano won gold at the Winter Games by the slimmest of margins.*

the Utah Jazz and Dallas Mavericks—also came down to a deciding seventh game on their home court.

James Worthy led the way in game seven of the finals with the first triple-double (double figures in points, assists, and rebounds) of his career, scoring 36 points, pulling down 16 rebounds, and dishing off 10 assists.

Night Games Come to Wrigley

For 74 years, the Chicago Cubs played by day—the way the game was intended to be played, at least according to purists. Only day games were played at Wrigley Field, the Cubs' home stadium (they also played on real grass,

1988

not artificial turf). But on August 9, Wrigley Field became the last Major League Baseball stadium to get lights, and night games could finally be played.

The 36,399 fans on hand were filled with mixed emotions, happy to be a part of history, but sad at the end of a proud tradition. The Cubs beat the New York Mets 6–4 in the first official Wrigley night game. The ceremony introducing the lights actually took place the night before, on August 8, as a 91-year-old Cubs fan flipped a switch to turn on the 540 lights that had been placed on the stadium's roof. But the game that night against the Philadelphia Phillies lasted only three and a half innings before it was postponed by rain.

After years of debate, the decision to put lights into Wrigley Field was finalized earlier in the year. The Cubs' management gave in to the economic reality that the franchise could fill the stand with bigger crowds for night games. However, only 18 night games were scheduled for the 1988 season.

Hershiser Sets Record, Gibson Blasts Homer

In his final start of the regular season on September 28, Los Angeles Dodger pitcher Orel Hershiser threw 10 shutout innings, bringing his streak of consecutive scoreless innings to 59 and breaking the big-league record set by Dodgers great Don Drysdale in 1968. Hershiser, who was just about unhittable over the final month of the season, won 23 games in all and captured the National League Cy Young Award.

Hershiser continued his dominance into the postseason. On October 12, he shut out the New York Mets 6–0 in the seventh and deciding game of the National League Championship Series, propelling the Dodgers into the World Series. In the Fall Classic, the Dodgers beat the Oakland A's in five games to become world champions. Hershiser won two World Series games, including another shutout in game two, then a complete-game victory in the deciding game five.

The great right-handed pitcher shared World Series heroics with teammate Kirk Gibson. In game one of the Series at Dodger Stadium against the heavily favored A's, the Dodgers trailed 4–3 with two outs in the bottom of the ninth inning. The A's had their ace closer, Dennis Eckersley, on the pitcher's mound, and it looked as if Oakland was going to jump out in front in the Series.

---

59 Shutout Innings

Here is how Orel Hershiser set a record for consecutive scoreless innings in 1988:

OPPONENT	SCORE	SCORELESS INNINGS PITCHED
Montreal Expos	4–2	4
Atlanta Braves	3–0	9
Cincinnati Reds	5–0	9
Atlanta Braves	1–0	9
Houston Astros	1–0	9
San Francisco Giants	3–0	9
San Diego Padres	0–0 *	10
Total		59

*Hershiser left the game after 10 innings with the score 0–0. The Dodgers lost the game in 16 innings.

Eckersley walked Mike Davis. Then, as the crowd stood and roared its approval, Gibson, sidelined with a serious knee injury, grabbed a bat and limped up to the plate. It would be his only at-bat in the series, but it was enough. Gibson, wincing in pain, smacked a 3–2 pitch into the right-field seats for a two-run homer that gave the Dodgers the victory and the momentum to take the Series.

Gibson added this dramatic homer to the one he hit four years earlier to help the Detroit Tigers win the 1984 World Series (see page 48).

NFL Suspends 19 Players for Drug Use

NFL commissioner Pete Rozelle wanted the message to be heard loud and clear: The league would not tolerate drug use, even by its top players. Rozelle announced that 19 NFL players were being suspended for substance abuse.

Among the 19 were defensive superstars Lawrence Taylor of the New York Giants, Dexter Manley of the Washington Redskins, and Bruce Smith of the Buffalo Bills. They were among 18 players who received 30-day suspensions. Tony Collins, a runningback for the Indianapolis Colts, received a one-year suspension.

NFL guidelines state that a player who fails a drug test for the first time receives a warning and treatment. If a player fails a second drug test, he is suspended for 30 days. A third failure results in a lifetime suspension, although the player may apply for reinstatement based on good behavior.

L.A.'s the Place *Hockey superstar Wayne Gretzky was dealt from the Edmonton Oilers to the Los Angeles Kings in a shocking trade.*

Oilers Trade Gretzky to Kings

Few cities have ever had a love affair with a professional athlete as intense as the relationship between NHL great Wayne Gretzky and the city of Edmonton, Ontario, in Canada. So it was a complete shock when Peter Pocklington, owner of the Edmonton Oilers, announced one of the most startling trades in sports history. Gretzky (along with two other players) had been traded from the Oilers to the Los Angeles Kings (for two players,

1988

three first-round draft choices, and $14.4 million). The details of the trade hardly mattered to Edmonton hockey fans. The Great One (as Gretzky was known) was leaving.

"It's like ripping the heart out of the city," said Edmonton mayor Laurence Decore. Hockey fans in the town agreed. In his nine seasons with the Oilers, Gretzky set 43 NHL scoring records, won eight consecutive Most Valuable Player trophies, captured seven straight scoring titles, and led his team to four Stanley Cup championships. No wonder Canadians felt as if their national treasure had been stolen from them by the United States.

As it turned out, Gretzky himself had requested the trade. In July of 1988, he married American actress Janet Jones. At the time, Canadian hockey fans treated their wedding like a royal affair, tuning in to the event on television and welcoming Jones into their extended "family."

When the trade was announced a month later, though, Canadians blamed Jones for stealing their superstar. Gretzky said Los Angeles offered him a new challenge, to make hockey popular in a city not known for its love of the sport. But he also moved to make it easier for his wife to pursue her acting career.

Gretzky wept openly at the press conference announcing his departure, but Pocklington accused him of acting for the cameras, stating that Gretzky had a huge ego, which is why he requested the trade. The Oilers' owner later refuted the claim, but the damage had been done. The greatest hockey player who ever lived was leaving the country of his birth and the city where he rewrote the NHL record book.

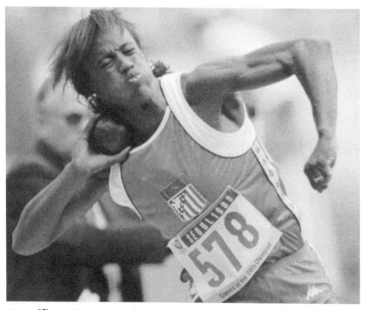

Magnificent Seven *Jackie Joyner-Kersee won the gold medal in the heptathlon—a seven-event competition to identify the world's best female athlete—with a record-setting performance at the Olympics.*

Sisters-in-Law Lead the Way at the Olympics

In some ways, they could not have been more different. Jackie Joyner-Kersee was all about hard work, muscle, and sweat, considered by many to be the finest female athlete of the second half of the 20th century. Her sister-in-law, Florence Griffith Joyner (known as "Flo Jo"), also a world-class athlete, combined her great physical abilities with a flashy style and fashion savvy. The two American women teamed up to dominate the track-and-field events at the 1988 Summer Olympic Games in Seoul, South Korea, in September. They combined to win five gold medals.

Joyner-Kersee broke her own world record in the heptathlon on her way to Olympic gold, shattering the rarely surpassed 7,000-point mark in the event by scoring 7,291 points, almost 400 points ahead of her nearest competitor. (The heptathlon is a seven-event competition made up of the 100-meter hurdles, the shot put, the high jump, the 200-meter race, the long jump, the javelin, and the 800-meter race).

She followed up her victory in the heptathlon by setting an Olympic record in the long jump, leaping an amazing 24 feet, 3 1/2 inches to earn her second gold medal. Until Joyner-Kersee did it, no one thought it was possible to win the grueling two-day heptathlon, and then come back and win an individual event. Bruce Jenner, the 1976 Olympic decathlon gold medalist, said of Joyner-Kersee, "She's the greatest multi-sport athlete ever, man or woman."

Flo Jo captured three golds. She won the 100-meter sprint, setting an Olympic record with a time of 10.54 seconds. In the 200-meter race, she set a world record with a time of 21.34 seconds. Her third gold medal came as part of the United States' 400-meter relay team.

The United States also was strong in the swimming and diving events. Seventeen-year-old Janet Evans set a world record on her way to winning the 400-meter freestyle swimming event. She also won gold medals in the 800-meter freestyle and 400-meter individual medley. Matt Biondi won seven swimming medals, including five gold.

Fashion Statements

In addition to her great athletic achievements at the 1988 Summer Olympic Games, Florence Griffith Joyner made some of the most memorable fashion statements of the 1980s.

From her catchy nickname (Flo Jo) to her glittering, sexy track outfits, from colorful, one-legged unitards to outrageous six-inch fingernails and make-up, Flo Jo was style personified. She made no apologies for breaking the rules of how a track star should dress, look, or carry herself.

Flo Jo later went on to design new uniforms for the NBA's Indiana Pacers.

American Greg Louganis became the first diver to win two gold medals in two consecutive Olympics. In 1984, at the Games in Los Angeles, Louganis won gold in the platform and springboard events. He repeated those victories in Seoul four years later. In 1988, his victory had added drama when Louganis hit his head on the diving board during a preliminary round of the springboard competition, but still came back to win the event.

Johnson Stripped of Gold Medal

In addition to the success of Jackie Joyner-Kersee and Florence Griffith Joyner, the United States picked up another track and field gold medal—although it didn't appear that way at first. Canadian sprinter Ben Johnson defeated his American rival, Carl Lewis, in the 100-meter sprint, running a world record time of 9.79 seconds. Lewis finished second with a time of 9.92. But three days later, Johnson was disqualified and his gold

1988

medal was taken away when he tested positive for ozolol, an anabolic steroid that was banned by the International Olympic Committee. Johnson was barred from competing on Canada's national team for life and was sent home in disgrace. The gold medal was given to Lewis, who had won four gold medals at the Games in 1984 (see page 47).

Johnson's fall from grace led to increased efforts to eliminate the use of performance-enhancing drugs in the Olympics. More rigorous testing was introduced. Not only were athletes tested immediately after competitions, but also, in some countries, random tests were performed throughout athletes' training periods.

Big-Screen Baseball

Two of the best baseball movies of all time were released in 1988. *Bull Durham*, starring Kevin Costner, Susan Sarandon, and Tim Robbins, was written and directed by Ron Shelton, a former minor-league baseball player. It tells the story of a career minor-league catcher

Greg Louganis: Secrets and Success

When United States Olympic gold medal diver Greg Louganis hit his head on the diving board during a preliminary round of the springboard competition at the 1988 Olympic Games, it took five stitches to close the wound. Louganis was very upset, not simply because of the injury, but because Louganis was HIV-positive—a fact only a few of his closest friends were aware of.

Had everyone there been aware of Louganis' illness, panic might have ensued. The pool would likely have been drained, the competition disrupted, and the diver himself exposed to scorn or controversy for putting others in potential danger. (In reality, the chlorine in the pool was enough to kill any virus that may have been shed in his blood.)

Louganis recovered from his fall and captured the gold medal in the event the next day, as well as a second gold in platform diving, but the experience shook him deeply. Louganis was gay, something else

only his closest friends knew. He retired from diving after the 1988 games. In 1994 at the Gay Games in New York City, he announced his homosexuality.

Hiding his homosexuality and his disease for years took its toll. "It's been so difficult with the secret, and asking people to keep the secrets," he said in his autobiography, *Breaking the Surface*, published in 1995. "I was feeling like a fake."

In the book he discussed being gay, living with the secret, and living with HIV. His openness led to a greater comfort with himself, and with his place in diving history. "Being gay and being in sports isn't supposed to mix," Louganis said. "I think I proved that wrong."

Three years later, the growing specter of AIDS in American society would find an even more familiar face when Magic Johnson, one of the dominant athletes of the 1980s, announced that he had tested positive for HIV, the virus that causes AIDS.

Other Milestones of 1988

✔ National League president A. Bartlett Giamatti was chosen to become the new baseball commissioner.

✔ Jose Canseco of the Oakland A's became the first player in baseball history to hit 40 homers and steal 40 bases in the same season.

✔ The Miami Heat and the Charlotte Hornets joined the NBA.

✔ The catcher's helmet was required in the major leagues for the first time.

✔ The first African-American referee in the NFL, Johnny Grier, made his debut.

✔ Nike's "Just Do It" ad campaign debuted, encouraging everyone to go for their dreams, emulate their sports heroes, and, of course, buy Nike shoes. The phrase quickly became a part of American popular culture.

Jose Canseco

who is asked to whip an up-and-coming pitcher into shape and to teach him the ways of the game.

Eight Men Out, directed by John Sayles, based on the book by Eliot Asinof, tells the story of the 1919 Black Sox scandal, which almost destroyed baseball. John Cusack played Buck Weaver, D.B. Sweeney played "Shoeless" Joe Jackson, and Sayles played writer Ring Lardner. The heavily favored 1919 Chicago White Sox lost the World Series that year, and subsequently were accused of being paid by gamblers to purposely lose. It led to player suspensions and to the appointment of the first baseball commissioner, Judge Kenesaw Mountain Landis, to rid the game of gambling's influence—which was considerable at the time.

1989

On the Air

By the end of the 1980s, the influence of television on sports in America was so strong that it had direct effects on the very structure of the games. Teams moved to new cities because the television markets were larger. Television revenue had become more important than the money collected from fans paying to get into the actual event. Filling the home stadium became less important than local television deals, which more than made up for empty seats.

Entire leagues were restructured and additional tiers of postseason games were added because they made for good television. People who might not follow a particular sport every day throughout the regular season did show an interest in the playoffs. So television gave them more playoff games, which, of course, meant more advertising revenue—charged at much higher rates than during the regular season.

The big television money led to even bigger sponsorship agreements and huge contracts, with dollars reaching into the previously inconceivable millions, for America's professional athletes.

Television's marriage with sports had humble beginnings. The first television broadcast of a Major League Baseball game was on August 26, 1939, when WSBX-TV aired the action between the Brooklyn Dodgers and the Cincinnati Reds at Ebbets Field in Brooklyn, New York. It was seen by a few hundred people watching the approximately 400 television sets in all of New York City. The Dodgers and Reds split a doubleheader that day.

By the 1950s, sports were a staple of television programming in the still relatively young medium. Friday night boxing matches and Saturday afternoon baseball games became regular parts of the lives of sports-loving Americans.

The 1960s saw big television money just starting to make its way into professional sports. The man most responsible for this was NFL commissioner Pete Rozelle, who brought his league into the television spotlight and into the hearts and living rooms of American sports fans. It was television in the 1960s that catapulted football ahead of baseball—the traditional American national pastime—as the most popular professional team sport in the country.

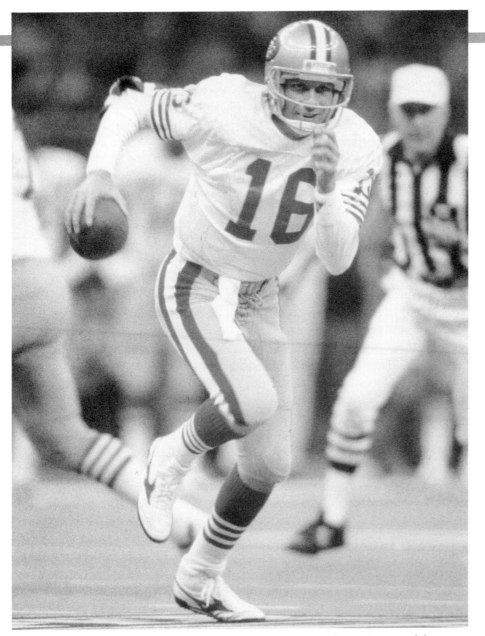

Joe Cool *Joe Montana helped make the San Francisco 49ers the NFL's team of the decade. He led his team to the winning score late in Super Bowl XXIII (see page 84).*

Rozelle's television contracts in the 1960s brought big money into the league. When CBS began televising NFL games in 1956, the network negotiated a separate contract with each of the 12 teams in the league. Each team got between $35,000 and $185,000 directly from the network for the rights to broadcast its games. In 1962,

1989

Rozelle worked out a package deal in which CBS paid the league $4.5 million dollars over two years for the rights to broadcast the games of all the teams.

In 1970, the television networks paid $50 million to broadcast NFL games. In 1985 that figure rose to $450 million. As the 1980s ended, the NFL signed four-year deals with CBS, ABC, ESPN, and Turner Broadcasting for a total of $3.6 billion. In the years between those early deals and the multi-billion-dollar contracts, the NFL expanded from 12 teams to 14, then 16, and finally 28.

In 1950, Major League Baseball signed a deal with the Gillette razor company for $6 million for the rights to the World Series and All-Star Games over a six-year period. Under the terms of the deal, Gillette ads would run exclusively on all television and radio broadcasts of the games. In 1970, the television networks paid $18 million for the rights to broadcast baseball, and in 1985 that amount had grown to $160 million. In 1989, baseball signed a deal with CBS for $1.1 billion, and another deal with ESPN for $400 million.

The huge, ever-expanding flow of money into the pockets of team owners and the leagues did not go unnoticed by the players. They began to demand their fair share of the revenue. Unions were formed, strikes were staged, and restrictive legal clauses binding players to teams for life were challenged and overturned in court. This led to free agency and bidding wars between teams, each club hoping to secure the top players by offering more than the competition. In the end, the players were big winners, commanding salaries unthinkable a few years earlier.

As the 1980s drew to a close, sports and television were as inseparable as a catcher and his face mask. Sports has always been a business, but with big television money leading to huge influence, the realization that in modern sports the bottom line was often of greater interest than the final score became an accepted reality.

Montana's Last-Minute Drive Wins Super Bowl

It couldn't have worked out more dramatically if San Francisco 49ers quarterback Joe Montana had written the script for Super Bowl XXIII himself. And, in a way, he did. The NFL's player of the decade led his team—the team of the decade—to its third Super Bowl victory, with a stunning, come-from-behind 20–16 win over the Cincinnati Bengals on January 22 in Miami.

Cincinnati's tough defense and a 93-yard, third-quarter kickoff return by Stanford Jennings helped give the Bengals the lead. San Francisco tied the score early in the fourth quarter on a 14-yard touchdown pass from Montana to his favorite receiver, Jerry Rice, but Cincinnati regained the lead on a 40-yard field goal by Jim Breech.

The 49ers trailed 16–13 with three minutes and 10 seconds on the clock and the ball on their own eight-yard line. It was time for Montana, one of the greatest quarterbacks in NFL history at working under pressure, to take things into his experienced hands.

Mixing pass plays and running plays, and working the clock with great skill,

Montana led one of the most exciting finishes in Super Bowl history. Using every second of time wisely, he moved the 49ers down the field 92 yards. The game-winning touchdown came on a 10-yard pass to John Taylor in the back of the end zone with just 34 seconds left in the game.

Montana set a Super Bowl record by throwing for 357 yards. And he wrote the latest chapter in his story as a clutch performer and a Super Bowl legend.

Lemieux Passes Gretzky

For the decade of the 1980s, any talk about the NHL naturally centered around Wayne Gretzky. Fans of hockey in the '80s were lucky enough to have watched the sport as its greatest player dominated the league.

As the decade drew to a close, however, a new star emerged. Twenty-three-year-old Mario Lemieux of the Pittsburgh Penguins won the NHL scoring title, finishing ahead of Gretzky for the second consecutive year. Lemieux, a 6-foot-4, 200-pound native of Montreal, Quebec, scored 85 goals and handed out 114 assists for a total of 199 points—the most ever achieved by anyone other than Gretzky. Along the way, he established himself as the league's best player.

Larger and stronger than Gretzky, Lemieux racked up nine hat tricks (scoring three goals in one game) in 1988–89 and set an NHL record by scoring 13 short-handed goals (when your team is short a player because of a penalty). Pittsburgh scored a record 118 power-play goals (when you team has one more play-

Cool Under Pressure

Sometimes all it takes is being told that you're not good enough. Joe Montana was not highly touted heading into the 1979 NFL draft. All he had done in college was work his way up from seventh-string quarterback for the University of Notre Dame to starter, lead the team in staging amazing late-game comebacks, and take the squad to the national championship in 1977.

But he never looked that good on paper. He was too skinny, he couldn't throw the ball all that far, and even his short passes looked a bit wobbly. He didn't have the sculpted body or rocket-launcher arm that seemed to be a requirement for modern quarterbacks. He was more of a throwback to the days of

Johnny Unitas, Len Dawson, and Bart Starr, all of whom played in the 1950s.

The San Francisco 49ers picked Montana in the third round of the 1979 draft. By his third year as a pro, he had become the 49ers' full-time starting quarterback. That season, he led San Francisco to a last-minute, come-from-behind victory against the Dallas Cowboys, the team that had dominated the NFL in the 1970s, in the NFC Championship Game (see page 26). He then won the first of his four Super Bowls.

There has never been anyone cooler under pressure. If there was time remaining on the clock and Montana had the ball, the 49ers always had a chance.

er than the opposition because of a penalty), and Lemieux was involved in 109 of those. His 199 points is the fourth-highest total in NHL history.

Giamatti Bans Pete Rose, Dies Eight Days Later

A. Bartlett Giamatti, former president of the National League, became baseball commissioner on April 1. A lifelong fan, devoted to baseball's traditions, Giamatti earned his reputation for being tough in dealing with unions as president of Yale University.

Giamatti spent most of his first five months as commissioner leading an investigation into the gambling activities of Pete Rose. Rose is baseball's all-time hits leader and was one of the game's best players for more than 20 years.

As a result of the investigation, a huge amount of evidence surfaced, chronicling years of gambling by Rose, including the devastating revelation that he had bet on baseball games. On August 24, Giamatti announced that an agreement had been reached banning Rose from any further involvement with the game of baseball.

Rose signed the agreement, which stated that he accepted the punishment without admitting nor denying his guilt. Rose was also allowed to apply for reinstatement into the game after a year, but Giamatti would give no guarantee that his position would change at that time.

This painful banishment immediately asserted Giamatti's power as commissioner, though it brought him no joy. Rose would have been a certain selection for baseball's Hall of Fame based on his performance as a player, and to this day he remains out of the Hall and banned from the game.

This sad series of events was immediately followed by a shocking tragedy that stunned the baseball world. On September 1, Giamatti died suddenly of a heart attack while at his summer cottage in Massachusetts—eight days after banning Rose from baseball. Giamatti was just 51 years old.

Earthquake Rocks the World Series

Certainly, 1989 was a very bad year for Major League Baseball. And there wasn't even a strike! August brought the lifetime ban of Pete Rose, and September began with the death of commissioner A. Bartlett Giamatti. Then, in October, a natural disaster struck the Bay Area just moments before game three of the World Series.

After beating the San Francisco Giants in the first two games of the Series at home, the Oakland A's headed to Candlestick Park in San Francisco for game three on October 17. A crowd of more than 60,000 fans had packed the stadium, eagerly awaiting their team's chance to get back into the Series.

At 5:04 p.m., the pre-game ceremonies were just getting started. Both teams were lined up on the field for the player introductions when the entire stadium began to shake violently. An earthquake measuring 6.9 on the Richter scale hit the entire San Francisco Bay Area.

Players and fans remained amazingly calm despite swaying press boxes and

The Day the Earth Shook *A massive earthquake rattled the Bay Area only minutes before the scheduled start of game three of the World Series at San Francisco's Candlestick Park. The Series resumed 10 days later.*

a sudden loss of power. Live television and radio broadcasts were temporarily knocked off the air. The ballpark held up to the stress, and no one inside was hurt.

Players scrambled to find their families. When broadcasts were restored, viewers who had tuned in for the game saw players holding their children and hugging their wives, all thoughts of a ball game replaced by concern for the safety of loved ones. Anxious fans in the ballpark waited for word of what to do next.

Baseball commissioner Fay Vincent, who had been in the job just a little more than a month, reacted quickly. He postponed the game and began emptying the ballpark before darkness set in.

As fans left the stadium, they had no idea of the extent of the devastation in the surrounding area. When the earthquake ended, 67 people were dead, and roads, bridges, and buildings had collapsed, causing billions of dollars of damage.

Suddenly, the all-Bay-Area World Series had lost its urgency, as people faced the more urgent tasks of rebuilding their city and their lives. Repairs were made to the stadium, and, although some called for the rest of the World Series to be cancelled, Vincent and San Francisco mayor Art Agnos eventually decided to resume the Series beginning October 27. The A's went on to complete their four-game sweep, although the games and final scores all seemed anticlimactic.

San Francisco Giants centerfielder Brett Butler put it best. "At the start, I realized what a privilege it was to be in the Series. Now, I realize what a privilege it is to be alive. When people think of the 1989 Series, they're not going to remember who won, but who survived."

1989

Shell Breaks NFL Coaching Color Barrier

In 1923, an African-American running back named Fritz Pollard became player-coach for the Hammond (Indiana) Pros of the NFL. This made Pollard the first black head coach of an NFL team, a position he held until 1925.

From that year until 1989, there were no black head coaches in the NFL. Then, in 1989, Art Shell, a 15-year veteran as a player for the Oakland Raiders and a member of the Pro Football Hall of Fame, was named head coach of the Los Angeles Raiders. Shell was the first black head coach of the modern era of football. Another professional sports color barrier had been broken.

Coaching Pioneer *The Los Angeles Raiders made Art Shell the NFL's first African-American head coach in 64 years.*

On October 3, with his team off to a 1–3 start, Raiders owner Al Davis relieved head coach Mike Shanahan of his duties and named Shell the new coach. Under Shell's leadership, the Raiders won seven of their next 10 games, although they failed to make the playoffs. (The next season, however, Shell's team went 12–4 and reached the AFC title game.)

Since Shell's appointment, there have been several other black NFL head coaches, including Dennis Green, Tony Dungy, Herman Edwards, and Ray Rhodes. Terry Robiskie served as an interim coach with the Washington Redskins for three games in 2000. Still, in 2003, there were only three black head coaches in the NFL: Dungy (of the Indianapolis Colts), Edwards (the New York Jets), and Marvin Lewis (the Cincinnati Bengals).

By contrast, the NBA hired its first black head coach in 1966, when future Hall-of-Famer Bill Russell became player-coach of the Boston Celtics. Between 1966 and 1989, when Shell broke the NFL coaching color barrier, the NBA had 18 black head coaches. As of 2003, there were 12 black head coaches in the NBA.

The first black Major League Baseball manager was hired in 1975, when Hall-of-Famer Frank Robinson became manager of the Cleveland Indians. Between that year and 1989, baseball had four black managers. As of 2003, there were four black major-league managers. There were also three Hispanic major league managers: Tony Peña of the Kansas City Chiefs, Carlos Tosca of the Toronto Blue Jays, and Felipe Alou of the San Francisco Giants.

Other Milestones of 1989

✔ Bill White was named president of baseball's National League. He became the first African-American to preside over a major sports league in United States history.

✔ Kareem Abdul-Jabbar retired from the NBA as its career leader in points (38,387), games (1,560), and minutes played (56,446).

✔ Greg LeMond won his second Tour de France bicycle race in July.

✔ Texas Rangers pitcher Nolan Ryan, baseball's all-time strikeout leader, fanned his 5,000th batter on August 22.

✔ Jim Abbott, a baseball pitcher with only one hand, played in the major leagues. Abbott went 12-12 for the California Angels.

Jim Abbott

✔ Triple Crown winner Secretariat, considered by many to be the greatest thoroughbred race horse of all time, died on October 4.

✔ On October 25, Los Angeles Kings star Wayne Gretzky passed Gordie Howe as the NHL's all-time leading scorer (1,852 points). Gretzky set the mark in Edmonton against the Oilers, the team for whom he had his greatest years.

✔ The International Amateur Basketball Federation opened the Olympics to all professional athletes, including those from the NBA. This led to "Dream Teams" of NBA stars competing in the Olympics in the 1990s.

✔ Chris Evert became the first tennis player, male or female, to win 1,000 singles matches.

Two Times Ninety

San Francisco 49ers wide receiver John Taylor became the first player in NFL history to score two touchdowns of more than 90 yards in the same game when he performed the feat in a Monday-night game against the Los Angeles Rams on December 11.

Taylor, the "other" receiver opposite Jerry Rice in San Francisco's powerful lineup, turned short passes from Joe Montana into touchdowns of 92 yards and 95 yards. He helped the 49ers rally from a 17-point deficit to win, 30–27.

San Francisco, playing under new head coach George Seifert (Bill Walsh's successor), won 14 games during the 1989 regular season. The 49ers went on to win their second consecutive Super Bowl by routing the Denver Broncos 55–24 in game XXIV on January 28, 1990, at the Superdome in New Orleans.

RESOURCES

1980s Events and Personalities

The 1980s (A Cultural History of the United States Through the Decades)
By Stuart A. Kallen (San Diego, California: Lucent Books, 1999)
This installment of the series looks at the 1980s—from politics to pop culture to rapidly emerging technology.

Jackie Joyner-Kersee
By Neil Cohen (New York: Sports Illustrated for Kids, 1992)
From modest beginnings, Jackie Joyner-Kersee rose to earn distinction as the world's greatest female athlete with her victory in the heptathlon at the 1988 Olympics in Seoul.

Nolan Ryan : Texas Fastball to Cooperstown
By Ken Anderson (Austin, Texas: Eakin Press, 1999)
Despite unparalleled success—including a record seven no-hitters—Nolan Ryan always remained one of sport's most humble and down-to-earth superstars.

We Were Champions: The 49ers' Dynasty in Their Own Words
By Phil Barber (Chicago: Triumph Books, 2002)
San Francisco built the team of the eighties in the National Football League, winning four Super Bowls and featuring such legendary players as quarterback Joe Montana and wide receiver Jerry Rice.

American Sports History

The Complete Book of the Olympics
By David Wallechinsky (New York: Viking Penguin, 2000)
An extremely detailed look at every Winter and Summer Olympics from 1896 to the present, including complete lists of medal winners and short biographies of important American and international athletes.

The Encyclopedia of North American Sports History
Edited by Ralph Hickok (New York: Facts On File, 1992)
This title includes articles on the origins of all the major sports as well as capsule biographies of key figures.

Encyclopedia of Women and Sport in America
Edited by Carol Oglesby et al. (Phoenix: Oryx Press, 1998)
A large overview of not only key female personalities on and off the playing field, but a look at issues surrounding women and sports.

ESPN SportsCentury
Edited by Michael McCambridge (New York: Hyperion, 1999)
Created to commemorate the 20th century in sports, this book features essays by well-known sportswriters as well as commentary by popular ESPN broadcasters. Each decade's chapter features an in-depth story about the key event of that time period.

Facts and Dates of American Sports

By Gordon Carruth and Eugene Ehrlich (New York: Harper & Row, 1988)
Very detailed look at sports history, focusing on when events occurred. Large list of birth and death dates for major figures.

The Sporting News Chronicle of 20th Century Sports

By Ron Smith (New York: BDD/Mallard Press, 1992)
A good single-volume history of key sports events. They are presented as if written right after the event, thus giving the text a "you are there" feel.

Sports of the Times

By David Fischer and William Taafe. (New York: Times Books, 2003)
A unique format tracks the top sports events on each day of the calendar year. Find out the biggest event for every day from January 1 to December 31.

Total Baseball

Edited by John Thorn, Pete Palmer, and Michael Gershman. (New York: Total Sports, 2004, eighth edition)
The indispensable bible of baseball, it contains the career records of every Major Leaguer. Essays in the front of the book cover baseball history, team history, overviews of baseball in other countries, and articles about the role of women and minorities in the game.

Total Football

Edited by Bob Carroll, John Thorn, Craig Neft, and Michael Gershman (New York: HarperCollins, 2000)
The complete and official record of every player who has played in the NFL. The huge book also contains essays on a wide variety of topics relating to pro football.

Sports History Web Sites

ESPN.com

www.sports.espn.go.com
The Web site run by the national cable sports channel contains numerous history sections within each sport. This one for baseball is the largest and includes constantly updated statistics on baseball.

Hickok Sports

www.hickoksports.com
Not the most beautiful site and devoid of pictures, but filled with a wealth of information on sports at all levels. It is run by Ralph Hickok, an experienced sportswriter, and is regularly updated with the latest winners.

Official League Web Sites

www.nfl.com
www.nba.com
www.mlb.com
www.nhl.com
Each of the major sports leagues has history sections on their official Web sites

Official Olympics Web Site

http://www.olympic.org/uk/games/index_uk.asp
Complete history of the Olympic Games, presented by the International Olympic Committee.

The Sporting News "Vault"

www.sportingnews.com/archives
More than 100 years old, The St. Louis-based Sporting News *is the nation's oldest sports weekly. In the history section of its Web site, it has gathered hundreds of articles on sports events, championships, stars, and more. It also includes audio clips of interviews with top names in sports from yesterday and today.*

INDEX